Raising
^a SCHOLAR

One Family's Journey

Jacqueline O. Ashe, EdD

Raising a Scholar: One Family's Journey
Published by Siblinks Publishing
Coram, New York

ISBNs:
979-8-9937049-0-6 (*paperback*)
979-8-9937049-1-3 (*eBook*)

FAMILY & RELATIONSHIPS / Parenting
EDUCATION / Parent Participation

Cover and Interior design by Victoria Wolf, wolfdesignandmarketing.com. Copyright owned by Jacqueline Ashe.

For my parents, who planted the
roots that shaped my life.

For my siblings, Cicely, SallyAnn, Vere, Barbara,
and Myra. My first circle, my lifelong friends,
and the ones who carried the story with me.

For Allison and Jason, who made the journey rich, meaningful, and unforgettable.

Contents

Introduction

Why I Wrote This Book

I still remember the soft ticking of the clock in our dining room as my father quizzed us on the capitals of the world. That table in our dining room, worn smooth at the edges from years of study sessions, wasn't just where we ate. It was where our minds were stretched and our confidence was built, one question, one conversation, one expectation at a time.

There were eight of us tucked into that three-bedroom wooden house: Daddy and Mommy, plus six children—five girls and one boy. From my perspective, we didn't have much in the way of money or luxury, but we had structure, storytelling, and a deep belief that education was our way forward. To me, it sometimes felt like we were just getting by. Even so, in the eyes of the villagers, we looked well off. My father owned several cars at a time when many families didn't even have one. Still, his hope was to open a business one day.

What truly set our family apart wasn't the cars or the house, but the values our parents instilled in us. They never pressured us to be perfect, but they expected us to strive for excellence. They made it clear that we were fully capable of achieving it. That expectation became our foundation.

Decades later, I look around and see how much the world has changed. Distractions are everywhere. Values shift faster than we can catch them. And school systems, especially in America, are not always built to recognize and nurture every child's brilliance. **The lack of recognition and support is especially evident for Black boys, who often carry the weight of society's low expectations.** Still, the dream remains that our children will rise, will blossom, and will surpass us in ways we never imagined possible.

That dream is the reason I wrote *Raising a Scholar: One Family's Journey.*

More importantly, I've lived that truth. You don't need wealth, private tutors, or Ivy League zip codes to raise a child who excels in school. What you need is presence. What you need is consistency. What you need is to believe in your child's future, even when the world sends mixed messages about who they are and what they can become.

Our son Jason went from chanting the alphabet in our small Bronx apartment to earning a PhD. We weren't perfect parents and we didn't have all the answers; we simply created a home that said, out loud and in quiet moments, "You are expected to do well. Mediocrity is not an option."

After he left for college, I returned to the classroom full-time and kept learning myself. Over time, I earned five degrees, including a doctorate. I didn't need them to be a good parent, but the process of raising a scholar awakened the one within me. I share this because persistence can turn ordinary effort into extraordinary outcomes.

This book is my testimony and my offering. It is proof that raising a scholar isn't reserved for the privileged few. Any parent, teacher, or caregiver who invests the time and nurtures curiosity can help a child grow into confidence and success. Every child carries the capacity to thrive, and every adult in their life holds the power to bring that promise to life.

But unlocking potential doesn't happen by accident. It happens through intention, love, and daily choices.

If you've ever asked yourself, "Am I doing enough?" this book will gently answer, "Yes, you are. And it's never too late to do more."

Within these pages, you'll find the strategies my husband and I used with Jason, as well as the methods I employed in the classroom with my students. But more than strategies, I hope you walk away with this truth: Raising a scholar is not about perfection. It is about purpose. It is about believing in your children, even when they doubt themselves. And it is about believing in yourself, even on the days when you feel unsure or overwhelmed.

This isn't merely a story about academic success. It is a story about faith in God, in growth, in grit, and in the greatness that lives in every child. It is also a reminder that while talent may be natural, scholarship is nurtured.

Because in the end, scholars are raised, not left to chance.

CHAPTER 1:

A Family's Quest for Knowledge

"Education is not preparation for life; education is life itself."

—JOHN DEWEY

BEING THE OLDEST OF SIX CHILDREN came with responsibilities that stretched far beyond chores. I was the first to speak in complete sentences, the first to recite the alphabet, the first to count to ten, and the first to cook a full meal all by myself by the time I was nine. But I also felt the weight of expectation, the responsibility to set an example.

My parents believed deeply in the power of education. For them, it was never just about grades or report cards. It came from a deeper place, especially for my father.

At fifteen, he had to leave school to help care for his family. He and his older sister lived with their grandparents after their mother married and moved away. Growing up in Antigua was not easy then, and challenges still linger today. My grandmother gave birth to her first child at the age of sixteen, and my father came along twenty-one months later. My grandfather worked in the sugarcane fields, and he had children with another woman in the same village. With more mouths to feed than money, survival took priority, and education slipped into the background.

Leaving school wasn't my father's choice. It was his sacrifice. Even as he worked under the blazing sun, the dream of an education stayed alive inside him. Whenever he spoke of those years, there was a sense of regret. However, there was also a resolution. He repeated the promise that became our inheritance: His children would continue where he was forced to stop.

By day, he worked the fields. By night, he studied through correspondence courses from Great Britian, learning to repair cars, exploring history, and following world events with remarkable insight. In him, I saw the strength of a self-taught scholar. For our family, education became the foundation of our lives.

Our First Classroom

Our home became a classroom long before the school bells rang. The dining table that held our meals transformed into a "center for learning." There, my parents taught us arithmetic, the alphabet, and eventually reading and writing.

After dinner, they pulled out books from the shelves: encyclopedias, a world atlas, a dictionary, and the *Guinness Book of World Records*. In our home, books weren't decorations; they were tools.

One of my favorite routines was naming the capitals of countries. Forgetting a capital didn't mean failure; it meant you had more to learn. We'd flip through the atlas with urgency, voices shouting the names of faraway places. That hunger for knowledge was planted in us like a seed, and it grew strong. To this day, I can spell C-Z-E-C-H-O-S-L-O-V-A-K-I-A in my sleep even though the country no longer exists.

Mathematics came with the same rigor. The times tables were drilled until they echoed in our minds like a familiar tune. My sisters Cicely and SallyAnn were especially quick with numbers, which is no doubt why my mother often took them to the market with her on Saturdays. Even now, they can calculate totals faster than most cash registers.

Not every moment was easy. My father's patience sometimes wore thin when we got answers wrong. His sternness stung, but now I see it differently. He wasn't being harsh for the sake of being harsh. He was just determined that his children would not waste their potential. He pushed because he believed.

Years later, when my husband Allison quizzed Jason on math facts at our dinner table, I smiled and said, "You're just like my father." He grinned and replied, "If it worked for us, it will work for him too."

Lessons in Time and Stories

Even the clock in our dining room became a teacher. Its hands moved slowly, ticking softly as we learned to tell time. It wasn't digital, so we had to study its face carefully, since mistakes were corrected firmly. That clock became more than a timekeeper. It was a symbol of discipline and focus.

Reading formed another pillar of our home. We devoured the *Nelson Phonics* readers, meeting Mr. Percy, Mr. Dan, Master Willie, and Dick and Jane. Those stories fueled our imaginations and sharpened our skills. Research confirms that strong early literacy experiences, especially phonics and interactive reading, set the stage for later success.

Every child in our home had a gift. Myra, the youngest, had the gift of performance. She recited, dramatized, and read aloud with a rhythm that drew an audience. She and our brother Vere often competed to see who could remember more or speak with more flair. Visitors had no choice but to stop and listen. Myra proved that age didn't define ability.

When Allison and I began dating, he often found himself the audience of one for Myra's and Vere's witty recitations. Their performances carried forward the spirit of learning that my parents had planted. Barbara, who's seventeen months older than Myra, was gifted with the Queen's English. The rest of us relished speaking in broken English. Barbara, however, was always "Miss Prim and Proper," even from an early age.

For my parents, education was about the pursuit of knowledge and about opening doors. Their dreams were built on sacrifice and hope, much like families everywhere who believe in the transformative power of learning. And they were right to believe it. Studies show that when families stay engaged through conversations, encouragement, and consistency, children are more likely to do well in school.

And then there was the guinep tree right in front of our home. Beneath its branches, we soaked up wisdom from our elders. There were no chalkboards, no classroom walls—only stories, questions, and lessons that shaped our worldview. That, too, was school. Looking back, I realize those moments mattered as much as any classroom. They reminded me that scholars aren't born by accident. They are raised with intention.

Defining a Scholar

The idea of raising a scholar is at the heart of this book. It isn't about raising straight-A students; it's about nurturing children who are curious, motivated, and open to growth.

A scholar is someone who delights in discovery, asks questions, and works hard at becoming a better learner. And that journey looks different at every stage of childhood. For younger children, being a scholar means showing curiosity, asking "why" and "how," and trying again when things don't come easily. In the middle grades, it means taking responsibility for learning, building habits of perseverance, and developing the ability to connect ideas. By the later grades, it means applying knowledge thoughtfully, seeking deeper understanding, and recognizing that learning is a lifelong process.

Many schools today use the word "scholar" to describe all students. During my years as an educator, I heard it often, spoken over intercoms and printed on bulletin boards yet seldom explained. To me, simply calling every child a scholar wasn't enough. Without understanding, it was simply a label. With understanding, it could become part of who they believe themselves to be.

What I want parents and caregivers to remember is that the responsibility for a child's learning should never rest entirely on schools. Classrooms can introduce knowledge, and homes reinforce curiosity. When families stay engaged, ask questions, model a love of learning, and nurture character, they shape a mindset that no system alone can build.

If there's one thing I know, it's that "scholar" isn't reserved for classrooms or for children with the highest grades. It's an identity, a way of seeing the world with curiosity and wonder. When families nurture that mindset at home, they hand their children a gift that lasts far beyond report cards. They give them a lifelong love of learning. Otherwise, it is like handing a child a key without ever showing them which door it unlocks.

I recall a quiet evening with Allison, when Jason was still a small child. As mothers worry, I asked, "Do you think we're giving him what he needs?"

Allison looked at me and said, "We're not just giving him what he needs. We're raising an independent thinker."

I saw proof weeks later when Jason traced countries on his placemat, paused, pointed at the globe, and asked, "Mommy, is Jamaica close to Africa?"

I smiled, amused by the curiosity behind the question. At that moment, I thought of my father, his eyes shining as he quizzed us at the dinner table. The flame had passed.

Lessons in the Margins

- Education begins at home, long before formal schooling begins.
- Stories of sacrifice, such as my father leaving school at fifteen, instill a sense of urgency and gratitude in the next generation.

- Being the "first" in a family brings both responsibility and opportunity.

- Raising a scholar is an everyday act of sending the message: "Learning matters here."

What Worked, What Didn't, and What Made All the Difference

What Worked

- Parents leading by example, reading, questioning, and learning together.

- Sharing family history that underscores why education matters.

- Sustaining high expectations and believing in learning as a mindset rather than a chore.

What Didn't

- Assuming kids understood the importance of school without connecting it to their lives.

- Focusing too much on grades without celebrating effort, curiosity, or process.

What Made All the Difference

- Watching my father's unfinished education become the fire that fueled my own path and, later, Jason's.

- Knowing that education was more than grades. It was about shaping identity and possibilities.

- Treating everyday moments as opportunities to learn.

Strategies to Cultivate Opportunity and Equity

What to Try at Home	Why It Helps	Example
Share family stories.	Reinforces identify, belonging, and purpose.	Tell your child how grandparents overcame barriers in school.
Model curiosity.	Encourages children to mimic what they see.	Read aloud together, ask open-ended questions, and explore new topics as a family.
Create a learning space.	Shows that learning is a valued and intentional part of home life.	Set up a cozy corner with books, art supplies, or science kits.
Celebrate effort, not grades.	Builds confidence, persistence, and a growth mindset.	Praise your child's effort rather than the final score on a challenging task.
Engage as a learning team.	Strengthens family bonds while making learning collaborative.	Cook, garden, or build something together and talk through the process.

CHAPTER 2:

The Foundations of Early Childhood Development

*"Education is the most powerful weapon
which you can use to change the world."*

—NELSON MANDELA

The Sacred Early Years

The early years of a child's life are sacred. They are filled with wonder, discovery, and the shaping of identity. What a child sees, hears, touches, and feels during these years becomes the framework for how learning unfolds, how relationships are formed, and how character develops. These moments are far from fleeting; they are the building blocks of empathy, intellect, and resilience.

Children do not simply sit back and observe the world around them. They soak it up like sponges. A cardboard box becomes a castle.

A spoon transforms into a drumstick for an imaginary drum set, tapping rhythms on pots and pans with uncontainable joy. A simple question, such as "Why is the sky blue?" is more than curiosity. It is the beginning of how children make sense of their place in a world that still feels new and full of possibility.

A child's imagination is wide open, and their emotions are tender and sensitive. Joy, frustration, wonder, or hurt can surface quickly and intensely. In those moments, children need comfort, reassurance, and steady care. Our role in these years is both humbling and sacred: humbling because their trust is complete, and sacred because we are shaping minds, hearts, stories, and futures.

Our Family's Beginning

Because we believed that a child's earliest years are sacred and formative, Allison and I were intentional about how we raised Jason. From the moment he could crawl, we filled his world with stories, music, color, and warmth. More than just wanting him to grow, we wanted him to flourish.

Our journey began in a modest apartment on the Grand Concourse in the Bronx. It was cozy, with walls that carried the sounds of traffic and the laughter of neighbors drifting through thin barriers. We squeezed Jason's playpen between the couch and the window. At night, the steady rhythm of traffic outside blended with our dreams for his future. That small apartment held big hopes.

As Jason began to walk and talk, we longed for more space for him to run, quiet nights for sleep, and schools that would see and nurture his gifts. We moved to a fifth-floor walk-up on Anderson Avenue so we could save for a house. Those stairs were brutal. Carrying groceries, laundry, or even Jason when he was tired left us breathless. To ease the burden, we scraped together enough for a washing machine and a small dryer. Each climb up those stairs reminded us that sacrifices were worth it because we were building toward something better.

Eventually, we reached a new chapter by building a home in Suffolk County, Long Island. There, Jason had room to run, dream, and continue learning. Both Allison and I had grown up with space to play outside. We remembered running barefoot in the grass, racing with siblings under the Caribbean sun, and letting our imaginations stretch wide. Those memories shaped our vision of what home meant. For us, beyond a roof over our heads, home was also an environment where childhood could blossom.

Early Sparks

By eighteen months, Jason recognized the letters of the alphabet. By age two, he was writing his name. His eyes lit with curiosity, eager to take in everything around him. Whether we were strolling through the neighborhood or walking through the shopping area, we pointed out colors, shapes, and letters on signs and storefront awnings. He would make the sound of cars rushing by and mimic the noises of animals we mentioned. Even before he had the words, his mind was active, connecting everything he saw and heard. At home, he would count blocks, sort his toys by color, and delight in the rhythm of learning.

Coming from the old school, we drilled a little here and there. But our goal was never rote memorization. We wanted learning to feel like play. We followed Jason's lead and stayed curious right alongside him. Storytime became sacred. We gave each character a voice and asked, "What do you think will happen next?" Reading aloud was not just about books; it was about sharing stories. It was about belonging.

One of Jason's favorite books was *The Velveteen Rabbit*. The edition we owned was more than words on a page. The soft fur on the bunny's ears, the textured pages, and especially the little mirror at the back made the story come alive for him. That mirror, far from just a novelty, gave Jason a way to see himself inside the story and to imagine that he, too, belonged there. For Jason, this was early literacy at its most powerful: sensory, emotional, and immersive.

We encouraged him to tell his own stories. He flipped through picture books and invented tales about superhero vegetables and magical buses. These playful narrations revealed how deeply he thought and how much he loved words.

Even though books were always within reach, oral storytelling remained a cherished tradition in our home. I often told Jason stories from my childhood in Antigua, about climbing trees for mangoes and guineps, how my mother taught me to make saltfish cakes, and the afternoons I spent watching my grandmother cook. By the age of eight, I had learned enough from those quiet lessons to make fried dumplings on my own. I still remember carrying her a sample, beaming with pride. I shared that story with Jason many times, and each time, his eyes lit up. He was not just listening; he was connecting.

These stories became bridges, threads linking generations, cultures, and experiences. They were proof that learning does not begin in school; it begins in the stories we tell and the love we share.

The Role of Parents and Caregivers

Our moments with Jason reminded us that presence and intention outweigh wealth or circumstance when it comes to learning. Every parent and caregiver carries the same sacred opportunity to shape a child's sense of wonder and self-belief.

We are our children's first teachers. I cannot stress this enough. Long before any classroom, children learn from us how to ask, how to listen, and how to care.

Parenting does not come with a manual. It is filled with joy, mistakes, pressure, and growth. I was not a perfect mother—far from it. I lost patience at times, and I rushed through moments I should have savored. Yet I kept showing up with presence, humility, and love.

Whether you live in a small apartment or a large home, presence matters more than perfection. Belief in your child, their voice, their questions, and their potential is how scholars are born.

The Power of Everyday Moments

Jason loved watching me cook. He would climb onto a chair to help stir pancake batter or count carrots while I chopped. One afternoon, as we unpacked groceries, he held up a tomato and asked, "Is this a fruit or a vegetable?"

That single question turned into a conversation about food groups, colors, textures, and seasons. It became a science lesson, a vocabulary lesson, and a bonding moment, all from one tomato in the kitchen.

The kitchen became our first laboratory. The supermarket turned into a scavenger hunt. Folding laundry became color-matching. Learning was not something we scheduled. Learning was something we lived.

Every moment offered an opportunity to connect and teach. It wasn't about perfection but attention. The simple act of answering a question or noticing a child's curiosity can open doors that lead to lifelong learning.

Windows of Opportunity

Early childhood is a window, wide open, but not forever. It is when the brain is most flexible and most eager to learn. Activities such as singing the alphabet, stacking cups, or building with blocks strengthen the pathways that support all future learning.

Jason grew steadily during this window because we stayed consistent. We met him where he was, celebrated his curiosity, and adjusted our approach whenever something didn't work.

Books were everywhere—on shelves, under pillows, in backpacks, even in the car. Some days, Jason listened quietly. On others, he squirmed, flipped ahead, or resisted. But we kept the rhythm going. Even a few minutes mattered.

I am aware that not every family has access to books, safe spaces to play, or time. That is why I strongly believe in programs that provide free, culturally relevant books and help parents recognize learning opportunities in everyday life. These efforts remind us that scholars are raised with intention and purpose.

Building a Strong Foundation

Early education is not about pushing children to "achieve." It is about giving them roots and wings. Finger-painting, dancing to music, and playing make-believe are more than games; they are also forms of expression. They build coordination, confidence, resilience, and joy.

Supervised sensory play, storytelling, and imaginative thinking helps wire the brain for courage, problem-solving, and persistence.

These experiences plant seeds of curiosity that grow over the course of a lifetime.

So, if you are wondering, "Am I doing enough?" know this: If you are showing up, you are. Jason's early years were built on intention but not on a rigid blueprint. They were built on choices, choices to be present, to nurture, and to believe.

The journey to raising a scholar begins in kitchens and backyards, in bedtime stories and whispered questions, in the grace we give ourselves and our children.

Lessons in the Margins

- Presence is more powerful than perfection.
- Curiosity is a spark; what we do with it shapes a child's world.
- Every home can be a place of learning, whether filled with books or full of questions.
- A child's early years are sacred soil. What we plant there takes root for a lifetime.

What Worked, What Didn't, and What Made All the Difference

What Worked

- Creating a learning-rich home filled with books, conversation, music, and movement made early learning a natural and joyful experience.

- Making everyday activities, such as cooking, playing, or walking, rich in language and math.

- Encouraging Jason's curiosity by treating questions as learning opportunities rather than interruptions.

What Didn't

- Expecting Jason's development to follow a straight line, forgetting that growth often comes in leaps and pauses.

- Letting my own desire to "measure progress" overshadow the joy of discovery.

What Made All the Difference

- Nurturing Jason's curiosity. His tomato question reminded me that when we notice what lights up a child, we create space for them to bloom.

- Realizing that consistency matters more than perfection.

- Embracing the truth that imagination is not separate from learning; it is the heart of it.

Strategies for Creating a Stimulating and Nurturing Environment at Home

Age Range	Focus	What to Do	Why It Matters
0–2 Years	Literacy	Read simple, colorful books each day. Use playful voices and sing familiar songs with rhythm and rhyme.	Builds language, listening, and early sound awareness.
0–2 Years	Numeracy	Count objects during play and include songs or books that highlight numbers.	Helps children notice patterns and connect numbers to daily life.
2–3 Years	Literacy	Point out letters in books, on signs, and around the home. Sing alphabet songs and use letter puzzles to make learning fun.	Familiarizes children with letters and builds a strong foundation for reading.
2–3 Years	Numeracy	Sort toys or household items by color, size, or type. Praise your child's sorting choices and observations.	Strengthens problem-solving, organization, and early math thinking.

CHAPTER 3:

Building Strong Foundations

> *"The most effective way to raise a*
> *nice child is to be a nice adult."*
>
> —L. R. KNOST

Early Literacy: Planting the First Seeds

I'll never forget one church dinner dance in the Bronx when Jason was just two years old. The pastor came over to our table, and Jason, looking up with a sparkle in his eyes, called out, "Heaven Amoko!" It was his sweet attempt at saying "Reverend."

The pastor bent low and asked, "And how are you, young man?"

With pride, I said, "He's now writing his name."

The pastor laughed. "No, that can't be."

So we grabbed a program from the church dinner dance. We handed Jason a pencil, and with small but confident strokes, he wrote his name, J-A-S-O-N, on the back. The pastor's eyes widened as he lifted the program like a prize. My son beamed, soaking in the moment, fully aware that he had just done something remarkable.

That memory of him writing his name isn't special because Jason proved something. It is special because it showed how encouragement and consistency grow into confidence. Children often surprise us with how much they can do when we create the space for them to try.

Even before Jason could talk, I was reading aloud to him. Babies can hear and recognize their mother's voice by the third trimester, and reading during pregnancy helps shape early language and brain development. I didn't need a study to convince me. I believed in the power of my voice to reach him, so I read every day, even if it was only for a few minutes.

When I started working at Time Warner, one of my first paychecks went toward purchasing the *Hooked on Phonics* program. When the box arrived, it felt like more than just a package; it was an investment in Jason's future. Allison and I took turns teaching the lessons, but before long, I handed them over to him. His calm patience balanced my eager push for results, making him the perfect teacher for that season.

Each day brought small victories and a few funny moments. One afternoon, Jason read "sun" as "sud." I laughed and said, "Close enough. A sud is just a baby sun learning to shine." He beamed, proud of his effort, and we tried again. Those moments reminded me that learning is not about perfection; it is about growing together with patience, laughter, and love.

The discipline my parents modeled became muscle memory

when it was my turn to support Jason's love of learning. Their structure taught me that excellence isn't enforced—it's cultivated through **consistency, patience, and belief.**

Numbers and Patience: The Math Journey

While reading was my forte, Allison brought numbers to life for Jason. He patiently taught him patterns and equations, turning math into something approachable.

Jason's strength in math was evident long before middle school. Numbers came easily to him, and he often solved problems in ways that surprised even us. By the time he reached middle school, he was already ready for more advanced work. He completed the Algebra I and II Regents while still there, paving the way for precalculus and, later, calculus in high school. He remained in honors classes throughout and graduated in the top 2 percent of a class of nearly 600 students. His success was the result of steady practice, curiosity, and encouragement—the same qualities that had shaped his early years.

I remember one evening when Allison offered help and Jason smiled, saying, "I've got it, Dad." Pride and a touch of sadness crossed Allison's face as he realized Jason no longer needed his guidance in the same way. Our boy was growing up.

Research supports what I witnessed firsthand. Children's early experiences with literacy and numeracy at home have a lasting impact on later achievement. What began with counting blocks and reciting times tables became the groundwork for advanced problem-solving and lifelong confidence.

Music: Finding His Voice

Jason's love for music began with a toy keyboard at the age of seventeen months. At first, he pounded the keys in toddler delight, but even then, something stirred. By six, he was ready for piano lessons.

I still see him at my sister Barbara's wedding in Antigua. He was about seven or eight, sitting at the piano in the church, his feet barely reaching the pedals. As his little fingers moved across the keys, the room filled with the sweet sound of music. When he was done, the guests clapped, and he burst into tears.

Alarmed, I bent down and whispered, "Why are you crying, honey?"

He couldn't put it into words. Jason was shy, and all the attention overwhelmed him. He had played through his fear, but when the applause came, it felt like too much. He buried his face against me, and I held him close.

That moment revealed something to me. Music wasn't solely a skill for Jason; it was a form of courage. Later, he transitioned from piano to singing, joined school musicals, and eventually directed the church choir at the age of fifteen. Watching him lead singers, some more than twice his age, filled me with awe.

Music didn't just expand Jason's creativity. It gave him discipline, courage, and the confidence to stand before others, even when his knees were trembling.

Sports: Lessons in Persistence

Jason was small when he joined his first basketball team in the Bronx, but determination made him stand tall. Sports became another teacher in his life.

When we moved to Suffolk County, he discovered tennis. The coach at his middle school saw promise and recommended that he take private lessons. It was a financial stretch, but Allison and I agreed it was worth the sacrifice. Saturday mornings became tennis mornings.

By ninth grade, Jason was on the varsity team. By his senior year, he had become a top player. His persistence showed me that talent might open the door, but effort and encouragement keep it open.

Art: A World of Imagination

At twelve, Jason began watching *The Joy of Painting* with his cousin, Chanti. Bob Ross's calm voice and talk of "happy little trees" drew him in like a gentle invitation. What began as a Friday afternoon pastime soon became part of our weekly routine, filled with the soft sound of brushstrokes and quiet concentration. Jason would sit close to the television, his eyes following every swirl of the brush as if it were magic.

Before long, he began painting his own landscapes—rolling hills, sunsets, and ocean views that reminded me of Antigua. He became especially skilled at capturing the eyes in waves, those swirling, watchful patterns that seemed alive with motion and depth. We bought paints, canvases, and brushes, and our basement slowly transformed into a small studio. The smell of acrylic and the sight of color-streaked rags became part of our home's rhythm.

By fourteen, Jason's paintings were displayed in two public libraries, and Channel 7 Eyewitness News even featured him. I still remember asking, "How does it feel to see your art in a library?"

He paused for a moment, smiled, and said, "It feels like my imagination got invited to be part of the world."

That response stayed with me. It reminded me that creativity is not a distraction from academics. It is an extension of them. Art teaches children to observe deeply, to find beauty in the ordinary, and to express what words sometimes cannot. It builds empathy, patience, and the courage to share one's vision. In nurturing Jason's creativity, I realized we were also supporting his ability to think, feel, and see the world through a scholar's lens.

Beyond Talent: Building Social Awareness

Raising Jason was about more than developing his gifts. It was about preparing him to see the world clearly and walk through it with both confidence and compassion. Children absorb everything—the tone of our voices, the words we choose, and even the silences between them. That is why parents must be intentional about what they model.

Sometimes it was as simple as saying, "Wouldn't it be boring if all flowers were the same color?" Little analogies like that became big lessons about fairness, respect, and diversity.

As Jason grew older, our church community became a powerful extension of these lessons. It was a place where he learned to serve, to lead, and to see others beyond surface differences. Through mentors and experiences that challenged him to think critically about justice and belonging, Jason began to connect his personal growth to a larger purpose. One of those opportunities came through a leader who saw his potential and encouraged him to participate in a program focused on youth leadership and social responsibility. The experience shaped him deeply, broadening his view of what education could do—not only for achievement but for impact.

During my teaching years, I saw firsthand what happens when children grow up without intentional exposure to learning beyond the classroom. I once taught a seventh grader in Brooklyn who struggled with the simplest vocabulary. Her mother confessed she didn't even know what her daughter enjoyed reading. Then she asked, almost hesitantly, if she should take her daughter and her twin sister to get library cards. I was stunned, though I kept my composure. That moment broke my heart. When parents are not actively involved in their child's academic world, children don't necessarily fall behind due to their lack of ability but because of limited support, exposure, and belief.

Lessons in the Margins

- Consistency matters. Daily routines like reading, practicing the piano, or playing tennis on Saturdays built Jason's confidence.

- Exposure broadens vision. Choirs, art shows, and leadership conferences opened doors he never knew existed.

- Values anchor growth. Respect, empathy, and fairness weren't abstract; they were lived daily.

- Parental involvement is irreplaceable. Teachers and coaches helped, but nothing replaces a parent's or caregiver's steady hand.

What Worked, What Didn't, and What Made All the Difference

What Worked

- Turning everyday life into learning opportunities.
- Encouraging Jason to try multiple interests, from art to tennis.
- Balancing encouragement with patience. Allison's calm made room for my drive.

What Didn't

- Pushing too quickly when Jason needed more time.
- Forgetting that skill doesn't always equal emotional readiness.

What Made All the Difference

- Treating mistakes as playful, not shameful.
- Offering Jason leadership opportunities early.
- Rooting learning in values, such as respect, empathy, and fairness, so achievement never stands alone.

Strategies for a Stimulating and Nurturing Environment

(Elementary to Middle Years)

Age Range	Focus	What to Do	Why It Matters
5–7 Years	Literacy and responsibility	Create a short daily reading time and invite your child to retell the story or draw a favorite part.	Builds consistency, focus, and comprehension while fostering ownership of reading.
6–9 Years	Creativity	Offer simple instruments or art materials and celebrate effort more than perfection.	Encourages self-expression, imagination, and confidence.
7–10 Years	Numeracy and logic	Use real-life math—measure ingredients while cooking or budget a small allowance together.	Connects math to daily experiences and strengthens decision-making.
8–12 Years	Social awareness	Join community or cultural events together and talk afterward about what your child noticed or learned.	Strengthens empathy, teamwork, and a broader worldview.
10–12 Years	Critical thinking	Discuss age-appropriate news, dilemmas, or stories and ask, "What do you think, and why?"	Builds reasoning skills and confidence in expressing ideas.

CHAPTER 4:

Navigating School Choices and Nurturing Lifelong Learning

"The function of education is to teach one to think intensively and to think critically. Intelligence plus character—that is the goal of true education."

—MARTIN LUTHER KING JR.

A Decision That Shaped the Path

When it came time to think about school for Jason, we wanted more than a building with classrooms. We wanted an environment that would challenge him, fuel his curiosity, and prepare him for a bigger world.

I remember when my cousin, already raising her children in Suffolk County, urged us to consider moving there. Her insights became the tipping point in one of the most critical choices we ever made as parents. Looking back, I realize how that decision, made years before I entered the classroom as an educator, quietly shaped Jason's path and deepened my understanding of educational inequity.

Years later, as a teacher in the New York City public school system, I saw firsthand what families in underfunded neighborhoods faced—crowded classrooms, outdated textbooks, and buildings covered in graffiti and scaffolding. Our move to Suffolk had been a privilege, one that not every parent could access. And Jason would one day see that contrast clearly for himself.

Building Blocks of Literacy and Numeracy

Children are born ready to learn. Many start recognizing letters or counting objects by age two or three. Some even begin to write simple words. But none of that happens in isolation. These skills develop from having conversations, access to books, and daily opportunities to explore.

As a special education teacher, I've taught many middle school students labeled with learning disabilities. Yet what I often observed led me to wonder whether some had been misdiagnosed. In several cases, their difficulties seemed rooted less in an inability to learn and more in limited early exposure. Many, it seemed, had grown up without the foundational experiences that make literacy and numeracy feel familiar and accessible. It appeared that no one had taken the time—or perhaps had the knowledge or resources—to lay those essential early foundations.

During my first year of teaching, I was placed in an eighth-grade self-contained classroom. The majority of the students struggled to read at a third-grade level. At the time, the school had a literacy specialist from Australia, and I remember one day approaching her in tears over my students' inability to read and write beyond that level. She said gently, "I know you're doing your best, and it's not your fault. These students have experienced years of neglect." Her words stayed with me. I was devastated that these eighth graders were moving on to high school without the ability to read or write with confidence. That moment deepened my understanding of how much early learning matters—and how hard it is to catch up when those foundations are never laid.

Several summers ago, I taught a spirited first grader who couldn't name all her letters or count to ten. Yet I noticed something remarkable—she could sing every word of a pop song and mimic entire dance routines from YouTube without missing a beat. That told me everything I needed to know. Her mind was capable; what she lacked were opportunities. Though she had been diagnosed with a learning disability, what she truly needed was *rich exposure*—moments that connect symbols, words, and numbers to the world around her.

Children don't fail to learn; they often lack the kinds of experiences that make learning come alive. Research suggests that early home literacy and numeracy experiences have a powerful and lasting influence on academic achievement. When parents and caregivers make learning visible through conversation, curiosity, and connection, they give their children a lasting advantage—the confidence to trust their own minds and the freedom to explore the world with wonder.

A Well-Rounded Routine

Looking back, I realize how much consistency shaped Jason's childhood—through music and in the way his weeks unfolded with purpose. Wednesdays were set aside for the steady discipline of piano lessons, where he learned that persistence creates harmony long before the notes do. Thursdays were for vocal training, where voice control taught him more than pitch; it taught him confidence. Fridays invited color and creativity through art classes that stretched his imagination and sharpened his attention to detail. Saturdays belonged to tennis, where every serve and return built his stamina, focus, and quiet determination.

In our community, we believed that keeping boys busy kept them out of trouble. But for us, it was about more than keeping Jason occupied. It was also about stretching his mind and widening his world. We wanted him to experience a life open to every possibility. So we made sure his days were purposeful and his interests varied. In the end, the routines gave him balance, taught him time management and resourcefulness, and helped him discover the quiet joy that comes from showing up with purpose.

Facing Bias and Building Empathy

As Jason grew, we knew he would encounter bias in many forms—racial assumptions, economic stereotypes, and misunderstandings born from fear. We could not shield him from every challenge, but we could prepare him to meet them with awareness and grace.

Books became one of our most valuable tools. We read stories that featured characters from a range of backgrounds, including families like our own and others whose experiences were very different from ours. For example, we might read about children growing up in rural farming communities, immigrant families finding their footing in a new country, or classmates navigating life with disabilities. Those stories opened our eyes to the many ways people live, love, and learn. Afterward, we would discuss what we read. I might ask, "Why do you think the character felt left out?" or "Have you ever seen someone treated unfairly?" Those simple questions helped Jason notice injustice without becoming bitter. They created space for empathy to take root, one story at a time.

In our home, learning was expansive. It included academics, but it also reached beyond them. It was about understanding people and the world around us. We wanted Jason to see that life is filled with both beauty and complexity, and that fairness is something to practice and to expect. Whether through books, music, art, or everyday conversations, we encouraged him to think critically, appreciate differences, and respond to others with kindness.

As a teacher, I saw how exposure—or lack of it—can shape a child's worldview. Students who read widely, travel beyond their neighborhoods, or engage with people whose lives differ from their own often develop a deeper sense of empathy. They learn to see differences as opportunities to understand humanity from many perspectives.

Empathy is more than an emotion; it is a skill that grows through curiosity, listening, and reflection. When children learn to look beyond themselves and truly see others, they develop both wisdom and humility. Those qualities, once nurtured, extend far beyond the classroom.

Just as parents and caregivers begin this work at home, teachers carry it forward in schools. More than instructors, they are guides who help children see themselves and others reflected in what they learn.

The Role of Teachers and Cultural Competency

Teachers are guides, role models, and, in many ways, the second environment in which children grow. Yet not all teachers are equally prepared to meet the needs of diverse classrooms.

Parents and caregivers can often sense a teacher's cultural awareness during conferences. Do they speak of children as individuals, or do they rely on generalizations? Do they see possibilities, or do they focus on limitations? Those small moments often reveal whether a child will be seen and valued or quietly pushed to the margins and overlooked, unheard and underestimated. Still, cultural understanding must be supported by systems that also value equity. A school's environment tells a story of its own. The books on its shelves, the faces in its hallways, and even the condition of its walls send messages to students about what, and who, is worth investing in. When those messages are inconsistent, children feel it long before they can name it.

In Jason's Suffolk County school, resources were abundant, yet staff diversity was limited. That imbalance, plenty of materials but few mirrors, was a reality we had to weigh. Although there were not many teachers who looked like Jason, we recognized that the school offered stronger academic opportunities and a more stable learning environment than others. We understood that representation and opportunity do not always come in the same package, and so we made a deliberate choice. Still, that decision came with responsibility. At home, we made it a point to talk about what diversity means, why it matters, and how to honor his identity even in spaces where it was underrepresented.

Many years later, when Jason visited my Bronx school while home from university, the contrast became real in a way that no statistic could capture. As we approached the building, he slowed his steps and looked up at the structure before us. The building was supported by scaffolding on every side, as if it were being held together by sheer will. Jason's eyes widened. "Mom, please tell me this is not where you work," he said quietly.

I nodded, my heart tightening. "It is," I replied. "This is where many children come every day, expected to learn and thrive."

We walked inside. The windows were streaked with grime, the hallways were dim, and the paint was peeling. The heaters clanged noisily even on mild days. Jason took in every detail, his eyes lingering on the cracked walls and the stacks of outdated textbooks piled in the corner. Finally, he spoke again, his voice low and thoughtful. "I thought I understood educational inequity in theory. But seeing this, it's different when you stand inside it. It's not fair."

That moment stayed with us. For Jason, it was the meeting of theory and truth. For me, it was a reminder of what I had always known: Resources and representation shape not just academic outcomes but a child's sense of dignity and possibility. And yet, even in schools where resources are scarce, I have seen children rise when teachers believe in them. That belief can transform the atmosphere of a classroom, turning scarcity into hope and potential into progress. Every child deserves that kind of belief, the kind that sees beyond what is lacking to what can still bloom.

When Parents and Caregivers Step In

If schools are the soil, then parents and caregivers are the gardeners. Teachers may plant, but parents and caregivers water, tend, and prune. As an educator, I learned that children with engaged parents and caregivers, even those in underfunded schools, made more progress than those whose remained uninvolved.

Too often, I have met parents and caregivers unfamiliar with their child's Individualized Education Program (IEP), unaware that they had the right to advocate for accommodations. That gap underscored a painful truth: Uninformed parents and caregivers can unintentionally allow schools to shortchange their children.

However, when parents and caregivers attend PTA meetings and conferences, and have intentional conversations with service providers, they become powerful advocates. They remind schools that accountability is not optional. Engagement bridges gaps that resources alone cannot fill.

Lessons in the Margins

- Every choice matters. From neighborhoods to schools to routines, decisions shape opportunity.

- Diversity is more than numbers. True inclusivity is visible in books, artwork, curriculum, and teaching practices.

- Parental advocacy is powerful. Schools may falter, but engaged parents push systems to do better.

- Learning happens everywhere; education goes far beyond the classroom.

- Raising a scholar is not about privilege. It is about presence. It is about seeing inequities clearly, equipping children to rise above them, and partnering with schools to create the best path forward.

What Worked, What Didn't, and What Made All the Difference

What Worked

- Moving to Suffolk County opened doors to better resources, mentorship, and opportunities.

- Daily learning woven into home life through books, conversations, and an abacus anchored Jason's growth.

What Didn't

- Believing that resources alone were enough.

- Overlooking how much representation and cultural competency mattered, especially with few teachers of color.

What Made All the Difference

- Staying engaged through church, school, and home, building a network of support around Jason.

- Turning inequities into lessons through consistent advocacy and presence.

Strategies for Parents

Strategy	Description	Example
Expose children to diverse experiences.	Introduce your child to cultural, social, and intellectual diversity through shared exploration and conversation.	Take your child to a museum, cultural festival, or library program that highlights different traditions and histories.
Foster empathy and social awareness.	Guide your child to understand and connect with others' perspectives and emotions.	Volunteer as a family at a food bank or community center to help children build compassion and gratitude.
Promote critical thinking.	Encourage your child to reason through social and ethical dilemmas by asking thoughtful questions.	Discuss current events together and invite your child to share their perspective.
Evaluate school choices wisely.	Look for schools that value inclusivity, representation, and opportunities for parental involvement.	Visit schools, talk with teachers, and ask about diversity in books, curriculum, and staff.
Engage with teachers and administrators.	Build respectful, consistent partnerships with educators to support your child's growth.	Attend conferences prepared with questions about how your child is learning and developing.

CHAPTER 5:
Raising Whole Children

"To be yourself in a world that is constantly trying to make you something else is the greatest accomplishment."

—RALPH WALDO EMERSON

Heart and Voice

Raising a scholar isn't merely about sharpening the mind. It is also about tending both the heart and the voice. Emotional intelligence (EI)—the ability to recognize, name, and manage one's own feelings while also considering the emotions of others—shapes the inner world of a child. Individuality—the courage to express their unique gifts and identity—shapes the outer world.

When these two forces grow together, children become resilient, confident, and compassionate. They learn how to stand firm in who they are while still reaching out to others. And they carry into adulthood not only a love for learning but also a steady sense of self.

Emotional Intelligence in Action

One spring Saturday, Jason and I spent the day at the Museum of Modern Art in New York City. We wandered from gallery to gallery, laughing about the pieces that puzzled us and admiring those that drew us in. The ride home on the Long Island Rail Road (LIRR) should have been uneventful. But a woman, upon entering the car we were in, suddenly shouted a racial slur at Jason. Her words were sharp, cruel, and unforgettable.

Jason's face fell. My heart clenched. For a moment, I froze. A couple nearby whispered, "Ignore her, she's drunk." But neither of us could. Words had been spoken, and they hung heavy in the air.

I did not respond right away. My adrenaline spiked, and for a moment I was ready to fight. But I stayed silent because I was hurting too. The words cut me as deeply as they cut Jason.

When we got home, I remembered an old saying I had passed down to him years earlier: *"Sticks and stones may break my bones, but words will never hurt me."* At the time, I had thought it was wisdom. Now, standing in the rawness of that LIRR moment, I realized how wrong it was. Words can hurt. They can scar.

That night, I told Jason the truth. *"I was wrong when I taught you that saying. Those words did hurt. And I should never have dismissed that pain of spoken words."*

That moment taught me that raising a scholar meant more than offering Jason strategies. It meant showing him that I, too, was still learning. EI is not a box to be checked off; it's a dynamic, evolving quality. It is a way of living and modeling growth.

At home, we often practiced emotional literacy at the dinner table. Almost every evening, I asked, "How was your day? What was the best part of your day? What was the hardest part?" These questions opened the door to honest conversations.

One night at the dinner table, Jason shared that a classmate had made a careless comment about something he had worked hard on. His eyes dropped to his plate. *"It hurt,"* he said quietly.

"What could you say if it happens again?" I asked.

He thought for a moment. *"Maybe, 'I worked hard on it, and I like it.'"*

That small response mattered. Jason learned he did not need everyone's approval to value his own work. On another night, he laughed as he told us how he had shared his lunch with a hungry classmate. Allison reminded him, "Kindness sticks with people. They remember it."

Piece by piece, these conversations built what I think of as Jason's "emotional backpack." It was the invisible set of tools he carried everywhere—naming feelings, standing firm, and showing empathy.

Individuality as Expression of Identity

As emotions shaped Jason's heart, individuality shaped his voice. From a young age, creativity became his way of expressing himself to the world. His earliest drawings filled our refrigerator, but we wanted him to know his art mattered beyond our home. One day, Allison and I had one of his paintings professionally framed. It cost more than I expected, but it sent Jason a lasting message: *Your work has value.*

As he grew, Jason's creativity opened doors to new experiences and confidence. Opportunities to share his work publicly allowed him to see that his imagination could inspire others. Whether through art, music, or performance, he learned that his gifts were not meant to stay hidden. Later, he began singing in community events, and by his senior year, he played the lead role in *The Pajama Game*. I remember sitting in the audience, watching him command the stage with both humility and joy, and feeling an overwhelming sense of pride.

These moments were more than extracurricular highlights. They were affirmations of identity. Each one helped Jason see that creativity and scholarship do not compete with each other; they complete each other. His individuality became a bridge between knowledge and expression, head and heart.

Research confirms what we experienced firsthand: Children with stronger EI are more likely to believe in their creative abilities, and individuality often strengthens that connection. When feelings are named and honored, self-expression flourishes. When creativity is supported, engagement deepens.

Breaking Boxes, Building Confidence

Too often, society tries to shrink children into narrow boxes: "Boys do not cry." "Girls are too sensitive." Jason was a deeply sensitive young man. He noticed when classmates were left out. He cried at sad movies. He spoke up when something was not fair. Some people dismissed him as "too soft."

But Allison and I saw his sensitivity differently. We told him, "Your feelings are not a weakness. They are your strength. Never be afraid of them." That affirmation changed everything. Instead of hiding who he was, Jason leaned into it. Over time, others came to admire his ability to listen, to empathize, and to lead.

When children are freed from stereotypes and encouraged to embrace their individuality, they blossom.

The Parents' Role: Advocate and Guide

It is tempting to think that parenting means simply cheering from the sidelines. But raising a scholar requires more than applause. We are guides, mentors, and steady companions.

Advocacy in our home was not just about grades; it was about opportunity. When Jason showed interest in a subject or skill, we made space for it to grow. Sometimes that meant finding instructors who could challenge him or carving out time in our schedule so he could explore a new passion without pressure. There were voices suggesting he should focus only on academics, but we knew creativity and curiosity were not distractions. They were part of the same foundation that fueled his learning.

Parenting is a balancing act. It means stepping in without taking over, creating opportunities without controlling outcomes, and being present without overshadowing independence. Sometimes it meant loud applause from the audience. At other times, it meant sitting quietly beside Jason, letting him think, reflect, or cry, and allowing space for his own discoveries.

The incident on the LIRR reminded me that guidance is not always about direction; sometimes it is about humility. Jason did not need perfection from me. He needed honesty. He needed to see that even parents can admit mistakes and keep growing.

Lessons in the Margins

- Feelings deserve to be named and heard.

- Words can wound, and healing begins with acknowledgment, not denial.

- Uniqueness is not a distraction from learning; it is an essential component of the learning process. It is the heartbeat of growth.

- Parenting is a balance. It means guiding without molding, and creating space without control.

What Worked, What Didn't, and What Made All the Difference

What Worked

- Encouraging Jason to talk about his emotions and affirming his individuality through art, music, and performance, giving him confidence and a strong sense of identity.

What Didn't

- Rushing to fix his feelings instead of sitting with them.

- Comparing his path to anyone else's.

- Overloading him with advice when he needed quiet.

What Made all the Difference

- Modeling growth.

- Apologizing when wrong.

- Celebrating his uniqueness and actively advocating for his passions, permitting him to be both tender and firm.

Strategies for Parents

Strategy	Description	Example
Identify emotions.	Teach your child to name and acknowledge their feelings in healthy ways.	Ask, "Are you feeling frustrated or disappointed?" after a setback.
Validate effort.	Celebrate persistence and growth rather than just results.	Frame a painting or applaud effort during a school play.
Create safe spaces.	Establish zones or routines where your child can express thoughts and emotions without judgment.	Use a journal corner, an art wall, or family dinner discussions for open sharing.
Encourage exploration.	Support your child in trying varied interests to discover what sparks joy and confidence.	Allow participation in both soccer and painting within the same year.
Model growth.	Admit your own mistakes and demonstrate resilience when things go wrong.	Say, "I was wrong earlier, and I see how that hurt you."
Advocate for opportunities.	Protect your child's creative and personal growth by ensuring time and access to enrichment.	Find a mentor, arrange exhibits, or balance academics with hobbies.

CHAPTER 6:
Fostering a Lifelong Love for Reading

*"The mind is not a vessel to be filled,
but a fire to be kindled."*

—PLUTARCH

Do you remember the bedtime stories that made your eyes heavy while your child's sparkled with excitement? Those moments remind us that reading is more than a task; it is an adventure. A book can soothe, ignite curiosity, and stir the imagination, all in one sitting.

Helping children fall in love with reading isn't about turning them into lifelong bookworms. It is about showing them that books can take them anywhere.

When I was growing up, reading became my own passport to wonder. I still remember nights when I stayed up long past my bedtime with a flashlight in hand, completely absorbed in *The Far*

Pavilions. Through its pages, I traveled to India. I could almost feel the heat of the desert, hear the distant bells of the marketplace, and sense the ache of forbidden love. More than entertainment, that story became an experience. It taught me that reading allows us to live many lives, to understand people and places we may never travel to or meet in person.

That same magic is what I wanted Jason to discover. I knew that if he could find books that captured his imagination, reading would never feel like homework. It would feel like a possibility.

In today's fast-paced digital world, where short videos and quick content compete for attention, cultivating a love for books can feel daunting. But it is not impossible. By creating the right environment, offering diverse options, and making thoughtful choices, reading can shift from a "have to" into a "can't wait to." Books remain some of the richest tools for building vocabulary, empathy, focus, and creativity. Whether children hold paperbacks, flip through graphic novels, or listen to audiobooks, the goal is the same—to spark curiosity and open doors to new worlds.

Meeting Children Where They Are

Think of books like vegetables. Some children devour them eagerly; others need encouragement. Just as presentation matters with food, customizing the reading experience makes a difference.

The key is starting with what excites a child. Dinosaurs, sports, outer space, or fairy tales can all be gateways into literature. Pairing stories with audiobooks, humor, or illustrations makes reading more approachable. When children are allowed to choose, they feel a sense of ownership over the experience, and that sense of choice often unlocks joy.

Jason loved *Highlights* magazine in his younger years. It offered him an adventure filled with puzzles, games, and creative challenges. As he grew older and busier, his fondness for reading began to fade. I tried rekindling it with the *Harry Potter* series. To my delight, he took to it instantly, diving headfirst into that magical world. For a time, the spark was back.

Then I made a decision that, though rooted in faith, dimmed that light. Around that time, I was listening to *Family Radio*, a Christian station that often guided my choices as a parent. One afternoon, a program warned that stories involving magic could draw young people away from godly values. It unsettled me. My Christian upbringing had taught me to be cautious about anything that seemed to blur the line between imagination and spirituality. Out of that concern, I quietly took the books away.

At the time, I thought I was protecting Jason. But in truth, I was letting fear guide me more than understanding. Was the story inappropriate for his age? Probably not. It was simply a world of wonder through a child's eyes. Years later, I regretted that decision. I realized that Jason's curiosity was never in conflict with faith; it was part of how he engaged with the world God created.

That moment taught me something lasting. When a child finds joy in reading, our role is to nurture that joy, not restrict it out of fear. The right book at the right time can ignite a lifelong flame for learning, even if we do not fully understand its light at first.

Embracing Different Formats

Today's children often feel more at ease with screens than with hardcovers. Instead of resisting this shift, we can use it to our advantage. E-books and interactive apps offer features such as built-in dictionaries, audio narration, and animations that enhance the reading experience. These tools don't replace traditional books, but they meet children where they are and invite them into stories in new ways.

At the same time, tactile experiences remain powerful. Pop-up books, textured pages, or even scratch-and-sniff editions appeal to kinesthetic learners, turning reading into a hands-on adventure. The key is variety—having multiple paths to engage the imagination.

Representation also matters deeply. Founder and president of the Children's Defense Fund Marian Wright Edelman once said, "You can't be what you can't see." When children encounter characters who look like them, sound like them, or live experiences that feel familiar, they begin to see their own stories as worthy of being told. Recent research confirms this truth—when books reflect diverse cultural backgrounds, children's literacy engagement, comprehension, and critical thinking are strengthened. A bookshelf that includes diversity, whether through *The Snowy Day*, *Last Stop on Market Street*, *Wonder*, or *Hidden Figures,* does more than entertain. It builds empathy, broadens perspectives, and roots children in a world where they truly belong.

Creating a Cozy Reading Space

A love of reading grows best in the right environment, and this doesn't require a home library. A pillow by the window, a blanket in a corner, or even a basket filled with favorite books can turn a small space into a sanctuary for stories. Good lighting, a touch of quiet, and a sense that "this is where we read" can make all the difference.

When Jason was young, his little nook of books gave him ownership over his reading journey. He could choose what to pick up, settle in, and disappear into a story. That sense of autonomy created momentum, making reading feel less like a task and more like an adventure. But above all, he enjoyed creating his own stories, which he also illustrated.

Making Reading a Shared Experience

Reading can be a solitary experience, but when shared, it becomes a cherished family memory. Whether through bedtime stories, reading aloud over Saturday pancakes, or starting a family book club, shared reading strengthens both comprehension and connection.

In fact, research shows that dialogic reading—a shared reading approach in which parents and caregivers pause to ask questions, encourage predictions, and talk about the story—leads to measurable gains in vocabulary, comprehension, and print awareness, especially for children who may be at risk for reading difficulties. Many parents and caregivers may not realize how powerful those small, interactive moments can be. Reading together, when it's truly engaging, multiplies the benefits.

A family book club, where each member chooses a story and leads the discussion, is another way to keep reading vibrant. Younger children can enjoy listening to picture books while older ones may guide conversations on more complex themes. These shared experiences not only build literacy skills but also deepen family bonds.

More than that, they plant something lasting. When children see that books have a place not only on shelves but at the center of a family's life, they begin to understand reading as more than homework or entertainment. It becomes an integral part of who they are, a source of curiosity, connection, and confidence that extends far beyond childhood. That is the gift every parent and caregiver can give—not simply teaching children to read, but showing them what it means to live as readers.

Lessons in the Margins

- A child's spark for reading can be fragile. One wrong decision, even with the best intentions, can dim their curiosity, while one supportive moment can fan it into a flame.

- Meeting children where they are, whether through comics, audiobooks, or chapter books, shows them that their interests are valued and respected.

- Representation in literature shapes not just imagination but identity. Books that reflect diverse voices and experiences allow children to see themselves and others more fully.

- Creating an environment that celebrates reading, no matter how simple, invites children to step into stories with joy rather than reluctance.

- Including shared reading time becomes more than literacy practice; it is a way to bond, laugh, and learn together as a family.

What Worked, What Didn't, and What Made All the Difference

What Worked

- Making reading an experience, not an obligation.

- Using *Highlights*, late-night stories, and book choices to make reading joyful and memorable.

What Didn't

- Pushing "educational" books too hard or removing stories that sparked curiosity. The lesson was clear: Forcing doesn't promote curiosity, joy does.

What Made All the Difference

- Creating a reading space that felt like his own and allowing free exploration. That sense of ownership turned reading into a personal adventure that kept curiosity alive.

Strategies for Nurturing Growth and Academic Skills

Strategy	Description	Example
Balance academics and life skills.	Blend school learning with practical, social, and emotional growth.	Involve your child in chores, budgeting, cooking, or leadership roles that build real-world confidence.
Encourage independent learning.	Give your child choice and voice in what they explore to foster curiosity and ownership.	Let them select a project topic and guide them through the research and presentation process.
Develop critical thinking.	Build reasoning through discussion, reflection, and problem-solving.	Assemble puzzles, have family debates, or analyze character choices in books and movies together.
Emphasize perseverance.	Celebrate effort as much as achievement to strengthen resilience and grit.	Praise determination and progress, not just the final outcome.
Foster a reading culture.	Make reading a visible and celebrated part of daily family life.	Create cozy reading corners, host family book clubs, or set aside shared reading time each evening.

CHAPTER 7:
Cultivating a Growth Mindset

"Success isn't a result of spontaneous combustion. You must set yourself on fire."

—ARNOLD H. GLASOW

Embracing the Growth Mindset

To raise a true scholar, cultivating a growth mindset is essential. Dr. Carol Dweck, in *Mindset: The New Psychology of Success*, explains that believing intelligence and ability can grow through effort is one of the most powerful ideas we can pass on to our children.

A growth mindset reframes learning. Mistakes become invitations instead of indictments. Setbacks turn into detours instead of dead ends. Effort is celebrated as the fuel for growth.

I remember the first time I picked up Dweck's book. I underlined passages and made notes in the margins because they resonated so deeply with my lived experiences as both a mother and an educator. Her words gave language to what I had already seen in Jason's life—persistence, practice, and an openness to learning mattered far more than being "naturally gifted." It was not about "Am I smart?" but instead, "How can I get better?"

When children adopt this way of thinking, they learn that intelligence is not a fixed trait. Instead, it stretches and deepens through effort, reflection, and persistence. This belief does more than improve grades. It equips children to approach life with resilience, adaptability, and confidence.

Using a Growth Mindset to Combat Stereotypes

Children do not grow up in a vacuum. They are constantly bombarded by messages—some spoken outright, others subtle—that shape how they see themselves. A young girl might hear that "math is for boys." A Black or Caribbean child may encounter assumptions that specific careers or advanced programs are out of reach. A child from a modest background might internalize the belief that Ivy League universities are only for the wealthy.

These stereotypes, if left unchecked, can limit a child's view of their own potential. A growth mindset disrupts these narratives. It reminds children that their abilities are not set in stone. Instead, their skills can be developed through curiosity, hard work, and perseverance.

I saw this firsthand in Jason's schooling. As one of the very few Black boys in his advanced classes, the stereotypes were always there. Sometimes silent, sometimes spoken aloud. Yet, with a growth mindset, he was able to see beyond those limitations. He understood that effort mattered more than perception, and that his place in those classrooms was not a gift but a reflection of his persistence and preparation.

When children believe they can grow, they are more willing to take risks in learning. They begin to raise their hands even when unsure of the answer. They encourage their peers, celebrate improvement, and recognize progress in themselves and others. Homes and classrooms that foster growth mindsets become places where stereotypes lose their grip and every child has room to rise.

Jason's Homework Battles

A growth mindset is rarely learned in an abstract sense. It comes alive in everyday struggles, like a math worksheet full of erasures.

When Jason was younger, he had a habit of rushing through his math assignments. His pages were smudged, numbers were uneven, and mistakes were common. Allison could not stand untidiness in schoolwork. Night after night, when Jason turned in something messy to be checked, Allison would hand it back with a simple instruction: "Redo it."

Jason groaned. "But I already finished!"

Allison stayed calm. "Then finish it again, this time the right way."

At first, Jason saw this as punishment. He muttered under his breath, his pencil tapping hard against the table, sometimes with tears forming in his eyes. But over time, something shifted. The act of redoing his work stopped feeling like punishment and started feeling like practice. Jason began to slow down, double-checking his answers and taking pride in turning in something neat and correct.

One evening, after reworking a set of problems, he looked at his clean page and said with a shy grin, "Well, at least now it looks like I know what I'm doing."

That moment was a turning point. He no longer feared mistakes. He understood that a redo was not about shame, it was about growth. Looking back, those homework battles were less about arithmetic and more about resilience, discipline, and developing a mindset that would serve him for years to come.

Practices That Build Resilience

Helping children develop a growth mindset takes time and effort. It is like building a muscle. Repetition, patience, and encouragement strengthen it over time. The following practices worked in our home:

Praise effort over results. "I'm proud of how hard you worked" became a regular refrain. It told Jason that persistence mattered more than a grade.

Share mistakes openly. When I took a wrong turn while driving, I didn't give up or get flustered. I drove ahead, found a safe place, and turned around. Jason learned that even adults make errors and that the best response is to stay calm and correct course. Mistakes, like detours, can still lead us where we need to go.

Ask reflective questions. At the end of the day, I would ask, "What challenged you today?" or "What did you learn from it?" Reflection helped Jason see that growth often happens quietly, in the spaces between effort and understanding.

Resilience is not something we hand to our children. It is something we model, nurture, and encourage.

Progress over Perfection

Our culture loves perfection—straight A's, flawless performances, unblemished records. However, perfection is not where growth typically occurs. Growth happens in the drafts, the redos, the smudges, and the attempts that do not quite work out.

Jason's journey as an artist illustrates this beautifully. When he first picked up a paintbrush, his work was unrefined. He smeared colors together, his proportions were off, and his early canvases bore little resemblance to the images in his head. Yet he kept at it. Canvas after canvas, sketch after sketch, he practiced. Over time, his hand grew steadier, his eye more precise.

One day, his work was displayed at the local library. Later, he was interviewed on the morning news about his art. I could hardly believe this was the same boy who once covered himself in streaks of paint. His growth did not come from chasing perfection but from embracing progress.

That lesson, that small, persistent steps create transformation, became a guiding principle not only for Jason, but for us as parents.

Celebrating Achievements the Right Way

Children blossom when they are celebrated, but how we celebrate matters. Too often, we label children as "gifted," "brilliant," or "a genius." While those words seem flattering, they create invisible pressure. A child praised only for innate talent may fear trying new things, worried they will lose their label if they fail.

Instead, the most powerful celebration is one that focuses on effort, strategy, and persistence. Did your child stick with a challenging problem? Did they try again after making a mistake? Did they ask a thoughtful question? Those are the moments worth cheering.

When Failure Shows Up

Failure, though painful, is one of life's best teachers.

Jason had been an exceptional student for most of his K–12 life. So, when he arrived at MIT, failure was foreign to him. During his first semester, he failed a chemistry exam. He called me in tears, his voice cracking with disappointment.

"Mom, I don't know what happened. I studied so hard, but I failed."

I took a deep breath, steadying my own emotions before responding. "Jason, it's okay to stumble. What matters is how you get up."

That conversation was not easy. My instinct was to comfort him, but I also wanted him to see failure for what it was—an invitation to grow. In the weeks that followed, he regrouped, adjusted his study habits, and learned to ask for help. He not only passed the class, but he also strengthened his resilience.

That moment taught us both something invaluable—failure does not have the final word. It is simply a step along the path of becoming.

Lessons in the Margins

- Growth is not a straight line. It is a winding path filled with lessons.

- Perfection is a mirage. Progress is what truly matters.

- Mistakes are not the enemy; they are the soil in which resilience grows.

- Children learn most when effort is noticed, valued, and celebrated.

What Worked, What Didn't, and What Made All the Difference

What Worked

- Encouraging Jason to see mistakes as opportunities.

- Praising his effort instead of his outcomes, building a foundation of resilience.

- Helping him view challenges as invitations rather than obstacles.

What Didn't

- Pressuring him to succeed too quickly. My urgency sometimes made Jason chase my standards instead of discovering his own, stifling his natural curiosity.

What Made All the Difference

- Shifting from perfection to progress. Celebrating effort, modeling mistakes, and showing that growth lives in the redo moments built both confidence and resilience.

Strategies for Cultivating a Growth Mindset

Strategy	Description	Example
Value effort over success.	Focus praise on persistence, process, and improvement rather than the outcome.	Say, "I'm proud of how hard you worked to solve that problem."
Embrace challenges.	Teach your child to see struggles as opportunities for growth and problem-solving.	Allow your child to wrestle with a challenging task before offering help.
Celebrate mistakes.	Show that errors are natural and essential steps in learning.	Ask, "What can we learn from this?" or share your own example of learning through error.
Encourage self-reflection.	Help your child develop the habit of reviewing experiences to understand what worked and what didn't.	Use journals or family reflection time to talk about lessons learned.
Model a growth mindset.	Demonstrate your own learning journey and openness to growth.	Share something new you're practicing or improving, and invite your child to do the same.

CHAPTER 8:

The Role of Mentorship

*"A mentor is someone who allows you
to see the hope inside yourself."*

—OPRAH WINFREY

Embracing Mentorship

Mentorship is one of the quiet forces that shape the lives of young people. Unlike formal teaching or structured parenting, mentorship has a way of slipping into a child's life naturally, through a coach, a teacher, a neighbor, or even a peer. Its influence is often underestimated, yet its effects can be profound and lasting.

At its heart, mentorship is about connection. It is about passing down knowledge while also showing a young person what is possible and, sometimes, reminding them of who they already are. Mentors stand at the crossroads of promise and reality, offering both encouragement and challenge.

Why Mentorship Matters

The African proverb, "A single hand cannot tie a bundle," speaks directly to the role of mentorship. Parents do so much to guide their children, and teachers pour countless hours into shaping young minds. But a child often needs additional hands, mentors who extend the reach of guidance and add depth to what is already being taught at home and in school.

A good mentor is not just an authority figure; they are also a trusted advisor. They are catalysts for growth, models of resilience, and voices of affirmation. They do not take over a child's journey but instead walk beside them, showing that challenges can be managed and dreams can be pursued.

Parents and caregivers are typically the first mentors, planting the seeds of values and habits that will shape their children's lives. But external mentors, whether coaches, professionals, older students, or trusted family friends, bring unique perspectives that reinforce or expand on those values. Sometimes, a mentor validates a parent's or caregiver's message by echoing it differently. Other times, they introduce fresh wisdom that a parent or caregiver might not have access to.

Stories of Mentorship in Action

One of Jason's earliest mentors outside of our family was his tennis coach, Mr. Batson. Mr. Batson was not flashy, nor did he push Jason with aggressive authority. Instead, he taught through patience and consistency. He showed Jason how perseverance pays off, in life as well as on the tennis court.

I remember how Jason would come home after a long practice and repeat to us the words Mr. Batson had shared about focus and strategy. In addition to becoming a stronger tennis player, he grew into a young man who could handle pressure with composure. Mr. Batson's mentorship resonated with Jason's temperament—steady, thoughtful, and even-keeled. That fit made all the difference.

Not long after, another mentor nurtured a different side of Jason's potential—his creativity. Mr. Parisi guided him in mastering pastels and in refining the delicate control of his hand. We first met Mr. Parisi through the owner of *Frame That Art* in Miller Place, where we had Jason's art framed. The owner noticed Jason's growing interest in art and made the introduction. Under Mr. Parisi's direction, Jason learned how to layer color with intention and bring depth to his work. Mr. Parisi often praised the way Jason's eyes came alive on the page, proud of how his technique had taken root. When Channel 7 Eyewitness News covered the library art show, he stood among the crowd, smiling and telling us Jason was one of his best students. His mentorship helped Jason see himself not only as a student but as an artist.

Later, mentorship appeared in another form. Jason had a peer mentor, a fellow student who was a year ahead of him in high school and excelled in physics. Jason had some struggles with the subject at first, but this classmate took the time to explain difficult concepts, share study strategies, and encourage him to keep going when the material felt overwhelming. As a teacher, I know the power of students explaining ideas in ways their peers can grasp—sometimes even better than adults can.

When that student was accepted into MIT, Jason's imagination opened wide. Suddenly, MIT was not an abstract dream. It was a tangible possibility. That mentor lit a fire within him, a fire that carried Jason to MIT himself and beyond to a doctoral journey.

This peer-to-peer mentorship demonstrated that guidance does not always come from adults. Sometimes it comes from those just a step ahead, making the path seem reachable.

These stories reflect the heart of mentorship. It is not always about structured lessons. It is about resonance, about meeting a child where they are and nurturing what is already within them.

Mentorship in Educational Environments

In schools, mentors often show up as teachers, counselors, coaches, or even older students. These relationships matter because school can be overwhelming, and children need trusted individuals who can guide them through both academic and social challenges.

A teacher who stays after class to encourage a struggling reader or a counselor who helps a student navigate peer conflict can be as impactful as any formal curriculum. Mentors inside the school system help with academic skills and also teach children how to navigate complex systems, advocate for themselves, and recognize their own strengths

Teaching children to value mentorship also equips them with the skills of self-advocacy. They learn that asking for guidance is not a sign of weakness but rather a sign of wisdom. They know how to prepare thoughtful questions, listen actively, and respect someone else's time. These skills will serve them well in classrooms, workplaces, and their future communities.

Sometimes mentors become advocates. A teacher might speak up for a child in a parent–teacher meeting, or a coach might write a letter of recommendation that opens doors to scholarships. These moments matter. They amplify a child's voice when it might otherwise be overlooked.

The Many Faces of Mentorship

Mentorship is not a one-size-fits-all model. It adapts and evolves to meet a child's needs.

- **Academic Mentorship:** A teacher guiding a child in literacy or math.
- **Peer Mentorship:** An older student showing a younger one how to navigate middle school.
- **Professional Mentorship:** A family friend offering career advice or internship opportunities.
- **Faith-Based Mentorship:** A spiritual leader or youth advisor guiding values and purpose.
- **Community Mentorship:** A neighbor or extended family member who steps in with encouragement and wisdom.

Each type of mentorship offers something different, and each can be transformative. A young child may thrive under academic support while a teenager may need a mentor who introduces them to career pathways or personal discipline.

In the Caribbean, mentorship often happened informally. Growing up, I remember older neighbors and villagers who would keep an eye on us, not because they were assigned to do so but because that was how communities worked. They corrected us when we strayed, encouraged us when we did well, and reminded us that the community's eyes were always on us. That sense of collective mentorship shaped many children into responsible adults.

The Dynamics of Mentorship

Mentorship is most effective when it is founded on trust and clear boundaries. Parents and caregivers can help facilitate initial introductions, ensuring the relationship is appropriate and aligned with the child's needs. Over time, mentor and mentee find their rhythm, how often to meet, what to focus on, and how to measure growth.

But mentorship is a two-way street. Mentors provide wisdom, encouragement, and accountability. Mentees must bring openness, gratitude, and a willingness to act on the guidance provided. When both sides invest, mentorship becomes not just a helping relationship but a transformative partnership.

The Impact of Mentorship on Achievement

Research confirms what we observe in practice: Mentorship significantly impacts outcomes. Mentored students are more likely to engage in class, persist through challenges, and pursue higher education. They develop confidence, improve time management, and build resilience.

Mentorship does not stop at academics. It cultivates emotional intelligence, teaching students to read situations, manage stress, and respond thoughtfully and effectively. It also builds networks, connections that can open doors to opportunities later in life.

Simply put, mentorship molds more than students; it shapes well-rounded human beings. Mentorship is not a luxury. It is a necessity for children to become resilient, capable, and inspired.

Lessons in the Margins

- Mentorship is less about teaching facts and more about inspiring character.

- Peer mentors can be just as influential as adult mentors.

- Communities thrive when mentorship is woven into everyday life.

- Teaching children to seek and value mentors equips them with lifelong self-advocacy.

- A mentor's influence often lasts far beyond the relationship itself.

What Worked, What Didn't, What Made All the Difference

What Worked
- Reflecting Jason's personality and reinforcing the values we lived at home: patience, perseverance, and curiosity.

What Didn't
- Assuming every mentorship would click. Some lacked connection or clarity, reminding us that mentorship depends on fit, not just availability.

What Made All the Difference
- Inspiring him to dream bigger and modeling resilience in the face of setbacks.
- Those lessons shaped the way he approached every stage of his life.

Strategies for Guided Mentorship Engagement

Strategy	Description	Example
Identify mentors.	Help your child find admirable adults who inspire curiosity, integrity, and excellence in areas of interest.	Highlight a mentor like Mr. Parisi, who taught Jason how to bring eyes to life in art.
Build relationships.	Teach your child how to communicate respectfully, express gratitude, and stay consistent in contact.	Encourage monthly check-ins or thank you notes to maintain connection with a mentor.
Explore types of mentorship.	Expose your child to formal, informal, and peer mentorship opportunities.	Compare a school mentorship program with guidance from a youth group leader.
Set goals together.	Guide your child in creating specific, measurable, and realistic goals within the mentorship.	Work with a mentor in science to design and complete a small project.
Encourage observational learning.	Promote learning through watching, reflecting, and imitating positive role models.	Observe how a mentor handles pressure or solves problems at work, then discuss what stood out.

CHAPTER 9:

Self-Advocacy and Resilience

"I learned a long time ago the wisest thing I can do is be on my side, be an advocate for myself and others like me."

—MAYA ANGELOU

Teaching Kids to Speak Up and Stand Strong

Helping children become strong, confident learners involves more than guiding them through homework. It is about enabling them to speak up, ask for what they need, and find their footing when life challenges them. That is what self-advocacy and resilience are all about.

When children learn how to express their needs and bounce back from challenges, they not only survive school but also succeed. These skills are not luxuries. They are essentials that carry into adulthood, shaping how young people handle college, careers, and even personal relationships.

I did not always understand that resilience grows through struggle. There were times I wanted to step in, smooth over Jason's challenges, and "fix" things for him. But each time I held back, I watched him grow stronger and more confident in his own voice.

Communication: The First Step in Self-Advocacy

When children learn to communicate clearly with teachers, it is like handing them the keys to their own success. They stop being passengers and start driving their own journeys.

One evening, when Jason was younger, he was frustrated with a math assignment. His voice trembled as he said, "I just don't get it." My instinct was to explain the whole problem. But I turned to Allison, the math expert in our home, and he said gently, "Tell me what you do know. Start from there."

Jason hesitated, then began to explain the first few steps. Slowly, his confidence returned. He realized he was not lost; he was just stuck on one part. That slight shift taught him the power of saying, "I don't understand this step. Can you help me here?"

Here is the essence of self-advocacy: teaching our children to maintain eye contact, use calm body language, and frame their needs with "I" statements, such as "I need more time on this" or "I'm having trouble understanding that and would like it explained again." These small habits build confidence and remind children that their voices have value in any setting.

And these tiny habits accumulate over time. They shape a child's identity as an active learner capable of directing their own education.

Navigating School Systems with Confidence

Even as adults, school systems can feel confusing. Think about course syllabi, grade portals, or codes of conduct. For children, the maze can feel overwhelming. But students who know how to ask questions and understand their rights become strong self-advocates.

I taught Jason to treat a syllabus as a roadmap, not just a paper handed out on the first day. He learned to track his assignments and grades in a folder so that if a mistake appeared, he could point to evidence. I also encouraged him to write short, respectful emails to teachers, such as, "Good afternoon, I am not sure if my paper uploaded correctly. Could you confirm?" And when something wasn't clear, I reminded him to ask thoughtful, clarifying questions like, "Can you give an example of how this will be applied?" These practices helped him take ownership of his learning and communicate with confidence and respect.

Practicing Advocacy at Home

Our home was the training ground. Jason and I had a very open relationship where he could share his thoughts freely, and I encouraged him to express what mattered to him.

I remember when he wanted to join a club that met twice a week. Instead of giving an immediate answer, I asked, "Why is this important to you? How will you balance it with your schoolwork?" Jason paused, thought about it, and explained how the club would help him build leadership skills while still keeping up with his assignments. That simple conversation showed him that making a case for something he wanted was a skill he could carry everywhere.

Even small moments mattered. If Jason wanted to stay up later on the weekend, I asked him to explain how he would handle his

responsibilities the next day. These were not tests. They were opportunities for him to practice using his voice. The message was always
the same: Your voice matters.

Turning Disciplinary Moments into Growth Opportunities

Over the years, I've had many conversations with parents who felt
discouraged when their child came home with a note or a phone call
from school. Those moments can feel uncomfortable, even embar-
rassing. But they do not have to define a child. When approached
thoughtfully, discipline can become an opportunity for growth—for
both children and adults.

During one parent–teacher conference, the mother of a seventh
grader told me I was the first teacher to ever make her feel appre-
ciated. She said it was the first time she had received positive
comments about her daughter. This struck me because, as a teacher,
I recognized the many challenges parents and caregivers face. My
goal was never to make anyone feel as though they were falling short
but to partner with them in supporting their children.

I have worked with students who struggled to manage their
emotions or behavior in traditional classroom settings. One student,
for example, would occasionally burst into laughter during lessons.
Rather than focusing solely on consequences, our team worked
together to understand what triggered those moments and to find
ways to help him channel his energy more productively. That experience reminded me that every behavior tells a story, and when adults
take time to listen, support, and guide, we help children develop
self-awareness and self-control.

Even children who are typically well-behaved encounter
moments when their dignity or confidence is tested. I recall a quiet

student whose father arrived for a disciplinary meeting that included several of his teachers. When the meeting began, the father sat down and said gently, "Tell me your side." The boy explained that he had felt picked on by classmates and had finally lashed out. His father's decision to listen first shifted the tone of the conversation. Together, the team worked with him to create a plan that helped restore his confidence and rebuild trust in the classroom.

Jason faced an incident that embarrassed him. He told me he went to a teacher to ask if she could make change for a twenty-dollar bill. Feeling nervous, he asked a classmate to go with him for support. Instead of responding with patience, the teacher turned to him in front of others and spoke in a way that made him feel small. Jason came home upset and said, "Mom, I don't like the way the teacher talks to me." My protective instincts rose quickly, and I wrote a note to the school.

That experience reminded me that every child, regardless of temperament, will face moments when their sense of dignity is tested. In those instances, advocacy takes different forms. Sometimes it means encouraging a child to use their own voice; other times, it means lending them yours until they are strong enough to stand on their own.

When a child comes home with a disciplinary note, a complaint, or even a story of embarrassment, here are a few steps to help parents and caregivers respond:

1. **Pause before reacting.** Take a deep breath before meeting your child with frustration or disappointment. Your calm presence helps set the tone.

2. **Listen with curiosity.** Ask your child what happened in their own words. Listening without immediate judgment communicates that you value their perspective.

3. **Separate the child from the behavior.** Remind them, "I love you, but your choices have consequences." This reminder helps children understand they are not bad people, even when they make mistakes.

4. **Collaborate with the teacher.** See the note, phone call, or concern as an invitation to partner with the teacher. Ask for specifics about what happened and how you can support your child at home.

5. **Turn mistakes or misunderstandings into lessons.** Help your child brainstorm what they could do differently next time, whether it is a change in behavior, more transparent communication, or respectfully practicing self-advocacy.

By reframing discipline and challenging moments as opportunities for growth, you address the problem in the moment while strengthening your child's ability to navigate future challenges.

Resilience: The Companion to Self-Advocacy

Self-advocacy does not stand alone. It walks hand in hand with resilience.

Jason did not earn straight A's by never stumbling. There were tough exams, missed opportunities, and disagreements with friends. But I noticed the difference between defeat and resilience was not in the failure itself. It was in the response.

We built resilience at home by asking three questions:

- What went wrong?
- What can we learn?
- What is our next step?

I modeled this too. When I faced setbacks, whether on the job or in my personal life, I did not hide them. Jason saw me frustrated at times, but he also saw me regroup and keep going. Children learn resilience not from our perfection but from watching how we recover.

For most of Jason's life, I was a student myself. I began college when he was just six months old and often took classes part-time while managing family life. It was not easy, but it showed him that learning and persistence do not end in childhood. In many ways, my journey became one of the strongest examples I could give him.

Over time, Jason began using those same questions for himself. When he received a lower grade than expected, he sighed, then said, "Okay, I need to review these chapters again." That was resilience taking root.

Lessons in the Margins

- Self-advocacy begins in small moments, such as asking for clarification, negotiating responsibilities, or writing an email to express your needs.

- Resilience grows when children view challenges as temporary setbacks, rather than permanent failures.

- Discipline issues, or even unfair treatment, can be reframed as opportunities for learning and growth.

- Sometimes advocacy means stepping aside so your child can speak; other times it means stepping in when their dignity is at stake.

What Worked, What Didn't, and What Made All the Difference

What Worked

- Encouraging Jason to advocate for himself, building his confidence and independence.

- Approaching discipline with openness and curiosity, helping him turn struggles into strengths.

What Didn't

Hovering too closely over Jason, stalling his growth.

- Responding defensively to teachers instead of listening first, which made it harder to understand their perspective and support Jason effectively.

What Made All the Difference

- Letting him try first, but being ready to step in when the situation was beyond his control.

- Acknowledging that parents and teachers need to treat discipline as a team effort. Partnership helps children see discipline as an invitation to grow rather than as a source of shame.

Strategies for Teaching Self-Advocacy and Resilience

Strategy	Description	Example
Model advocacy.	Demonstrate how to ask for help respectfully and confidently.	Share a workplace story where you requested support or clarification.
Role-play real scenarios.	Practice self-advocacy in safe, low-pressure settings.	Have your child pretend to ask a teacher for extra help or clarification.
Encourage open dialogue.	Create regular opportunities for honest conversations about school and emotions.	Check in daily about challenges, progress, or social interactions.
Build emotional vocabulary.	Teach your child to name, understand, and manage their feelings with words.	Use feeling charts, emotion cards, or stories to discuss emotions together.
Guide problem-solving.	Walk your child through resolving conflicts and finding fair solutions.	Help them brainstorm ways to address a sibling disagreement or peer issue.
Reframe discipline.	Treat mistakes or complaints as opportunities for learning and reflection.	Listen first, then help your child plan a better response or decision next time.

CHAPTER 10:

Navigating Peer Pressure and Social Dynamics

*"I am not a product of my circumstances.
I am a product of my decisions."*

—STEPHEN COVEY

Recognizing the Pull of Peer Influence

As children move into adolescence, their social world expands quickly. Suddenly, being accepted by friends can feel just as important as doing well in school. That shift is a regular part of growing up, but it also introduces new pressures and quiet doubts. It is not our role as parents to shield our children from every influence but to help them stay rooted in their values, even when the crowd seems to be moving in a different direction.

You have likely heard the saying, "You are known by the company you keep." During the middle and high school years, this saying becomes especially true. A child who once seemed steady may suddenly shift, changing how they dress, the music they listen to, or their performance in school. Sometimes these changes are harmless explorations of identity. Other times, they may signal that your child is being pulled by peers whose choices do not align with the path you hope for them.

As parents and caregivers, our first task is to pay attention. Abrupt shifts in mood, behavior, or academics can be early indicators that a peer group is exerting pressure on a child. Instead of rushing in with warnings, it is better to create space for conversation. Children who know their home is a safe place to talk are far more likely to share when something does not feel right.

Ask about their friends. Listen closely to both the words they say and the feelings that surface between them. These open conversations act as an early alert system, allowing you to step in gently and guide your child before unhealthy influences take root.

Building Confidence from the Inside Out

One of the strongest shields against negative peer pressure is healthy self-esteem. A child who feels secure in their worth is far less likely to chase after the fleeting approval of others.

Self-esteem, however, does not grow overnight. It develops from consistent messages of support, encouragement, and belief in a child's abilities. In practice, those messages show up when we celebrate effort as much as achievement. A "B" earned through hard work deserves as much recognition as an "A" earned easily. When children understand that their value lies in persistence, integrity, and character rather than in accolades alone, they begin to see themselves through a wider, more resilient lens.

In our home, Allison and I made it a point to remind Jason that he didn't need to be like everyone else to succeed. We praised his academic drive, celebrated his individuality, and guided him to seek out friendships with peers who shared his curiosity and respect for learning. Because we consistently built him up and reinforced that he did not have to follow the crowd, peer pressure never took hold. Instead, he grew to understand that he was a leader in his own right and that others could look to him as an example.

Self-esteem is also shaped by what children observe in us. When they see us handle setbacks with dignity, criticism with calm, and rejection with perspective, they learn to do the same. Modeling confidence, even in the face of challenges, teaches them that resilience is not about never stumbling but about learning how to rise again.

Social Media: The New Peer Circle

Peer pressure no longer stops at the school doors. With the rise of social media, it follows children into their bedrooms, appearing on the screens they scroll through. Platforms like Instagram, Snapchat, and TikTok can amplify insecurities by presenting filtered images and curated lifestyles that often fail to reflect reality.

For young people, the constant comparison can feel relentless. Researchers have found that exposure to these idealized online portrayals can lower self-esteem and increase anxiety among adolescents. The highlight reel culture makes it easy for children to believe they are falling behind or do not measure up.

The nonstop comparisons and false images children encounter online are exactly why conversations about social media matter so deeply. These talks are about setting limits on screen time, but also about helping them make sense of what they see. We can explain how filters, editing tools, and performance shape many posts into something designed to impress rather than reflect real life. Just as importantly, we can encourage them to invest more in face-to-face friendships and experiences, where authenticity and trust matter far more than likes or views.

When children recognize the difference between reality and illusion, they are better equipped to navigate their digital world without letting it dictate their self-worth.

Encouraging Healthy Friendships

Friendships are a training ground for life. Through them, children learn about loyalty, honesty, respect, and empathy. Not all friendships, however, teach the proper lessons. Parents and caregivers can play an essential role by guiding without dictating.

The best way to begin is by modeling healthy relationships in your own life. Show kindness, resolve conflicts respectfully, and set boundaries with grace. Let your children see what good friendships look like in practice. Then, encourage them to seek peers who share their interests and values.

When Jason was younger, we frequently discussed the kind of people he should surround himself with. We encouraged him to look for friends who respected his goals and treated others with kindness. One day, he told me he had stopped hanging around with a boy who had started picking on others to get laughs.

"I did not want to be part of that," he explained.

I nodded, proud. "It takes courage to walk away," I told him. "And it says a lot about who you are becoming."

That moment stayed with me. It reminded me that teaching our children to evaluate friendships is one of the greatest gifts we can give them. It helps them protect their own integrity, even when social pressure runs high.

Helping Children Handle Pressure in Real Time

Knowing peer pressure exists is one thing. Responding to it in real time is another. Children need simple, practical tools to say no without feeling embarrassed or isolated.

Role-play conversations at home. Give them easy responses like:

- "That is not for me."
- "I am good, thanks."
- "I do not want to get in trouble for that."

These short, confident replies can help them step away without escalating the situation.

It also helps to discuss consequences openly. Every choice comes with outcomes, some of which are positive and some of which are not. When children see how short-term decisions, such as drinking at a party, can have long-term effects, such as health risks or lost trust, they gain perspective.

For single parents, offering this kind of guidance may seem more challenging. Balancing work, home, and monitoring friendships can be overwhelming. Even so, short, intentional conversations make a difference. A five-minute check-in can give a child the courage to resist pressure when it comes.

Shaping Healthy Social Habits

Beyond teaching children to resist negative influences, we also need to help them reflect on the company they keep. Encourage them to ask themselves:

- Do I feel good about myself after spending time with this friend?
- Do they respect my choices and boundaries?
- Do I feel pressured to act in ways I dislike when I am with them?

These reflective questions build critical thinking about relationships. Pairing these questions with opportunities to practice healthy friendships through volunteering, team sports, youth groups, or clubs gives children real-world chances to make informed choices and build confidence in their social skills.

Lessons in the Margins

- Peer pressure is powerful, but preparation is even stronger.
- By encouraging open conversations, modeling confidence, and guiding children toward positive friendships, we help them navigate social dynamics while maintaining their own identity.
- Children flourish when they know their worth is not up for negotiation.

What Worked, What Didn't, and What Made All the Difference

What Worked

- Encouraging Jason to reflect on his friendships and how he felt after spending time with peers

- Reinforcing the value of positive influences taught him that being true to himself mattered more than fitting in.

What Didn't

- Waiting too long to step in when peer choices conflicted with his values.

- Hesitating to intervene meant some lessons were learned the hard way.

What Made All the Difference

- Holding regular, open conversations about peer pressure, social media, and friendships.

- Giving him language to set boundaries and confidence to walk away strengthened his sense of self.

- Monitoring his social media activity, providing insight into the influences shaping his world.

Strategies for Navigating Peer Pressure and Social Dynamics

Strategy	Description	Example
Encourage open communication.	Foster honest, judgment-free conversations where your child feels heard and supported.	Ask your child daily how their day went and listen without interruption or immediate advice.
Build self-esteem.	Reinforce your child's confidence, uniqueness, and sense of self-worth.	Praise effort, highlight strengths, and celebrate individuality through affirming words and actions.
Teach decision-making.	Guide your child to think critically and weigh pros and cons of their choices.	Discuss examples such as comparing attending a party with preparing for an important test.
Create supportive spaces.	Connect your child with peers and environments that promote positive growth and belonging.	Enroll them in sports teams, youth groups, or creative clubs that align with their interests.
Set healthy boundaries.	Teach your child how to say no confidently and to respect others' boundaries in return.	Role-play phrases like, "That's not for me" or "I'd rather not do that."

CHAPTER 11:
Educational Pathways and Transitions

"Educating the mind without educating the heart is no education at all."

—ARISTOTLE

Moving into Middle School: A Pivotal Transition

Moving from elementary to middle school is like crossing a pivotal bridge in a child's educational journey. This transition is not only about changing classrooms or stepping up in academic rigor. It is a profound metamorphosis that shapes the academic, social, and emotional layers of a child's life.

The middle school years are filled with both challenges and opportunities. Expectations rise, the environment shifts, and the rhythms of daily life change. Beyond what children learn in school, this stage profoundly influences who they are becoming. That is why, as parents, caregivers, and educators, we must lean in with intention. The way we guide children through middle school can either equip them with resilience and vision or leave them vulnerable to drift.

Addressing the "School-to-Prison Pipeline" Phenomenon

One of the most troubling realities associated with middle school transitions is what scholars refer to as the school-to-prison pipeline. This pattern shows how students, especially those of color and those with disabilities, who face suspensions or expulsions often end up entangled in the criminal justice system.

The school-to-prison pipeline is not an abstract policy issue. It is about real children whose futures are altered by systemic inequities. For many students, middle school becomes more than an academic milestone. It can serve as a tipping point between promise and derailment.

Parents, caregivers, and educators must remain vigilant. We can advocate for restorative rather than punitive approaches to discipline, push back against zero-tolerance policies, and normalize open dialogue about fairness in parent–teacher meetings and school board forums. Speaking up for equity is one of the most powerful ways we keep opportunities alive for every child.

When Jason entered middle school, I paid close attention to how discipline was handled. I was not looking for excuses for misbehavior. I was looking for assurance that mistakes would be treated as learning opportunities, not life sentences. That kind of vigilance is what helps dismantle systemic inequities, one school community at a time.

Preparing for Academic and Social Changes

Middle school is often the first point where academic pathways diverge. Students may be placed in advanced classes, introduced to electives, or asked to carry heavier workloads. Expectations rise, homework multiplies, and grades begin to hold more weight.

At home, we established an after-school routine that prioritized homework while also allowing for rest. Having a predictable routine helped Jason build confidence and taught him how to balance competing demands.

But academics were only half of the story. The social landscape of middle school was unpredictable. Friendships shifted overnight. Cliques formed. Puberty added an entirely new layer of emotional complexity.

It was in this season that I realized the importance of regular check-ins. Jason needed a safe space to discuss more than just grades. He needed to process the pressures of friendship, belonging, and identity. Sometimes I offered advice. Other times, I simply listened. Both responses were equally powerful.

By giving attention to both academics and social-emotional growth, parents and caregivers can create an environment where children not only survive middle school but also thrive.

Importance of Parent–Teacher Engagement

The transition from having one primary teacher in elementary school to several teachers in middle school requires a new level of parent and caregiver involvement. Suddenly, your child has six or seven different adults shaping their learning, and each one sees a different slice of who they are.

Today, technology makes staying in touch easier, since most schools now offer online portals that allow parents and caregivers to check grades, assignments, and attendance. Even so, online access cannot replace the impact of personal conversations with teachers.

When Jason was in school, we never missed any conferences. At the time, email was just starting to become common, but most parents still relied on handwritten notes or phone calls. I preferred writing letters since it felt more personal than the new digital forms of communication and helped keep the connection genuine. I did not join the PTA, as I worked in New York City and attended classes after work; however, I remained as engaged as possible through conferences and written communication. That consistency sent Jason a clear message: His education was a priority.

Even when schedules are demanding, parents and caregivers can still maintain a connection. A note, a phone call, or a meeting at school helps strengthen the partnership between home and the classroom. The form of communication matters less than the message itself: Children are supported by both their teachers and their families.

Instilling Self-Regulation and Time-Management Skills

If there is one skill that middle school demands most, it is the ability to manage time and emotions.

For Jason, heavier workloads could have been overwhelming. However, by teaching him how to prioritize, breaking down big projects into manageable steps, using planners, and setting aside consistent time for study, he developed independence and confidence.

Self-regulation extended beyond academics. It also included learning to control emotions when friendships grew rocky or when grades were not as high as he had hoped. We often reframed setbacks as stepping stones, reminding him that failure was never final. It was feedback.

These skills, including time management and emotional regulation, prepared him for middle school and for the long path ahead.

Lessons in the Margins

- Middle school is not just about academics. It is about shaping identity.

- Equitable discipline practices safeguard opportunities for students who might otherwise slip through the cracks.

- Changes in social life are just as significant as those in academic life, and both deserve equal attention.

- Parent/caregiver–teacher collaboration creates a network of accountability and support.

- Resilience, time management, and emotional control are foundational skills that carry into adulthood.

What Worked, What Didn't, and What Made All the Difference

What Worked
- Recognizing the academic and social shifts middle school brings.
- Using structured routines, regular conversations, and teacher check-ins to build confidence and consistency.

What Didn't
- Overlooking the emotional toll of social dynamics.
- Focusing on academics while underestimating the weight of friendships and peer pressure.

What Made All the Difference
- Viewing middle school as a time to nurture both academics and emotional growth. Supporting Jason holistically helped him balance schoolwork with social challenges and develop true resilience.

Strategies for Managing Educational Transitions

Strategy	Description	Example
Identify transition points.	Recognize key stages where your child may need additional guidance and reassurance.	Support your child through changes such as moving from elementary to middle school or adjusting to a new environment.
Encourage adaptive skills.	Promote resilience, independence, and flexibility to help your child adjust smoothly.	Teach time management, organization, and self-advocacy to meet new expectations.
Engage in early exposure.	Introduce your child to new stages or settings before transitions occur.	Arrange school visits, orientation days, or opportunities to shadow older students.
Enhance communication.	Maintain open and consistent dialogue between students, caregivers, and teachers.	Schedule regular progress meetings or check in frequently to discuss challenges and successes.
Utilize technology and resources.	Leverage digital tools and community supports to make transitions smoother.	Use educational apps, parent portals, or academic planners to track assignments and communication.

CHAPTER 12:
Exploring and Nurturing Interests

"Do not go where the path may lead, go instead where there is no path and leave a trail."

—RALPH WALDO EMERSON

Discovering and Cultivating Passions

Every child has sparks of curiosity waiting to be fanned into a steady flame. Our job as parents, caregivers, and educators is to notice those sparks and give them room to grow. When a child gets excited about something, whether it's a science project, a musical note, or a basketball court, learning no longer feels like work. It feels like discovery. A textbook turns into a treasure map, and a homework assignment becomes an opportunity to stretch a new skill.

This type of engaged learning is not just poetic language; it is a genuine approach to learning. It is how the brain works.

Neuroscientists have shown that when children care about what they are learning, their brains hold onto the information more deeply. In other words, emotion and passion fuel memory and growth. If we want children to flourish, we cannot leave their curiosity untended.

Nurturing Specific Interests That May Lead to Scholarships

Middle school is an excellent time for discovering specific interests that may even lead to scholarships down the road. Whether a child shows an ear for music, a gift in math, or athletic talent, these skills can blossom into future opportunities if they are nurtured from an early age.

That type of nurturing might look like signing up for a summer workshop, encouraging participation in a local contest, or enrolling in a program that offers expert guidance. Beyond skill-building, these experiences give children confidence and stories to tell when it is time for scholarships or college applications.

I learned an important lesson about balance when Jason was in the second grade at St. Philip Neri Catholic School in the Bronx. I told him that our trip to Busch Gardens depended on how well he did on a test. I thought I was motivating him, but I ended up putting pressure on him. Jason grew so anxious that he second-guessed himself and kept changing his answers. His teacher noticed and gently informed me of what she had observed. That moment stopped me in my tracks. I realized I was pushing him in a manner that chipped away at his confidence rather than building it.

From then on, I shifted. Instead of tying rewards to performance, I focused on encouragement. I began planting the idea of scholarships as early as age two, not as pressure but as a possibility. I would discuss with him how scholarships could make college more affordable and how hard work could open doors. Over time, Jason took ownership of that vision. He did not see scholarships as my dream for him but, eventually, as a goal he could attain on his own.

That realization reminded me that when we support a child's goals, we must do it with hope not fear. Encouragement fuels confidence, while pressure stifles it.

Encouraging Extracurricular Involvement

Extracurricular activities are powerful. They teach teamwork, responsibility, and perseverance in ways a classroom alone cannot. Whether it is drama, sports, band, or debate, these activities help children discover who they are outside of academics.

But balance matters. At one point, I signed Jason up for too many things, thinking more would make him well-rounded. Instead, he became tired and stretched to the limit. That experience taught me that balance, not busyness, leads to real growth.

Research supports this idea. Learning scientists remind us that opportunities outside the classroom, particularly when supported by caring adults, help shape not just what children know, but also who they become. When extracurriculars are chosen with care, they become a pathway for growth rather than just another item on the calendar.

The Role of Community Service and Civic Engagement

Community service is one of those quiet forces that shape a child's heart. Volunteering at a food pantry, cleaning up a park, or helping out at a nursing home does not just look good on a résumé. It builds empathy.

Too often, families stop at the school's required service hours. But going further by letting children participate in causes they genuinely care about teaches them to see themselves as part of a bigger world. Attending a town hall, organizing a fundraiser, or joining an advocacy group shows them that their voice matters. And when children connect their passions to service, they realize their gifts bless others in addition to themselves.

Encouraging Specialized Skills and Talents

Every child brings something unique to the table. Some are quick with numbers, others have a natural rhythm for music, and still others can sketch a picture that takes your breath away. The challenge for parents, caregivers, and educators is to make sure these gifts are not overlooked or dismissed but are celebrated and nurtured.

That kind of development might involve finding a mentor, pursuing advanced courses, or entering a competition that allows a child to showcase their skills. Just as important is recognition. When children see their abilities honored, they lean into them with even more confidence. The message is clear: "This is worth pursuing. You are good at this."

Lessons in the Margins

- Passion is fuel. When children are allowed to follow their interests, motivation rises naturally.

- Balance matters. Too many activities can drain energy rather than build it.

- Service shapes scholars. Community involvement builds empathy and broadens perspective.

- Recognition empowers. Celebrating a child's gifts motivates them to grow.

- Guidance nurtures; pressure stifles. Encouragement plants seeds, but pressure pulls them up too soon.

What Worked, What Didn't, and What Made All the Difference

What Worked

- Supporting Jason's passions early, whether in academics, sports, or music, helping him see the value of pursuing what he loved.

- Celebrating his strengths and giving space to explore, building both confidence and curiosity.

What Didn't

- Overbooking him with too many activities in the name of balance. That approach left him drained, reminding me that downtime and focus matter as much as opportunity.

What Made All the Difference

- Allowing Jason to explore freely, guided by passion rather than pressure.

- By separating success from rewards or fear of failure, he developed a lasting love of learning.

Strategies for Encouraging Exploration and Nurturing Interests

Strategy	Description	Example
Encourage exploration of new interests.	Create an environment where trying new hobbies is welcomed, supported, and celebrated.	Introduce your child to a community art class, science club, or dance program.
Diversify experiences.	Promote participation in a wide range of activities to broaden your child's skills and worldview.	Encourage involvement in different sports, music genres, or volunteer projects.
Offer continuous support and feedback.	Provide ongoing encouragement and constructive feedback to sustain motivation and growth.	Discuss progress and challenges regularly, such as after each new music or language lesson.

CHAPTER 13:
High School Transitions and College Prep

"The future belongs to those who believe in the beauty of their dreams."

—ELEANOR ROOSEVELT

The College Journey Begins

The shift from high school to college is one of those seasons that families never forget. There is excitement, worry, and plenty of late-night conversations about what the future holds. For parents and caregivers, it is a time to step into the role of guide and cheerleader. For students, it is about learning to stand on their own, test out their interests, and dream a little bigger.

This stage is not merely about filling out forms or choosing classes. It is about identity and growth. It is about helping our children figure out who they are becoming, not just what they are studying. I remember this clearly, as we walked alongside Jason through his own college process. From financial aid forms to campus visits, from sending out music recordings to choosing the school that felt right for him, we lived the ups and downs of this journey together. And along the way, we learned lessons that I hope will ease the path for other families.

Exploring Career Paths and Building Connections

High school, more than simply a stepping stone to college, is a transformative experience. It is a chance for students to try out who they might want to be. That could mean shadowing a professional, picking up a part-time job, or volunteering in a field that sparks their interest. Sometimes, a few weeks in a real-world setting can tell a student whether they are on the right track.

Relationships matter here too. A teacher's encouragement, a mentor's advice, or even a parent's introduction can lead to opportunities students might not find on their own. Today, connections also grow online. Platforms like LinkedIn enable students to follow individuals in careers they admire and even connect with alums from schools they are considering. Those early steps in networking help students see what is possible.

Choosing High School Classes with College in Mind

One of the trickiest aspects of preparing for college is determining which high school courses will make the best impression. It is tempting to load up on the most challenging classes, but balance is key. A future engineer may need advanced math and science, but adding a creative elective can show versatility. An aspiring artist should absolutely shine in their creative subjects, but core academics still matter.

Research even suggests that a student's GPA, earned through consistent effort across subjects, is a stronger predictor of college completion than test scores. That is encouraging, because it means steady work and good habits over time carry more weight than a single high-stakes exam.

Scholarships, Aid, and the FAFSA Hurdle

If there is one topic that makes families anxious, it is money. The world of scholarships and financial aid is crowded with deadlines, forms, and fine print. It can feel overwhelming, but starting early makes all the difference.

I remember Allison and I sitting at our kitchen table with Jason's FAFSA application spread out in front of us. Because it required our financial information, it was a team effort. We triple-checked everything, and although it wasn't glamorous, it mattered. That process taught me that parents are more than mere bystanders in this journey. We are active participants.

And the research backs this up. Studies show that when families get help filling out the FAFSA, students are more likely to enroll in college and stay there. Financial support does not just get students in the door; it keeps them there.

The Application Season

There is nothing quite like senior year when the applications start rolling. Jason applied to eleven universities. That meant keeping spreadsheets, checking deadlines, and proofreading essays late into the night. He was accepted to eight schools and waitlisted at three. Each "yes" and "maybe" came with its own set of possibilities and hard choices.

We encouraged Jason to apply broadly, even to schools he was unsure about, just to keep his options open. But the part I loved most was helping him showcase who he was beyond the numbers. Jason was a gifted musician and artist, and we did not want that side of him to get lost in a pile of GPAs and test scores. He recorded a song he had composed, burned it onto CDs, and sent them with his applications. He also created a glossy portfolio of his artwork.

That personal touch worked. To our surprise, the Boston Conservatory at Berklee reached out, even though Jason had not applied there. It was a reminder that colleges are looking for whole people, not just grades. When students show their talents and passions, unexpected doors open.

Campus Visits and Fairs: Finding the Right Fit

Visiting colleges was one of the most eye-opening parts of the process. Jason quickly discovered that prestige did not always equal excitement. At Harvard, he found the endless brown buildings uninspiring. At Brandeis, even with a full scholarship offer, he felt no real connection. Pittsburgh's city vibe did not appeal to him, and Yale and Cornell did not spark much interest either.

But then there was MIT. It was not just about the academics, though the rigor was unmatched. Jason felt energized by the atmosphere, the people, and the possibilities. MIT was not the easiest choice, but it was the right one.

Campus visits offer more than brochures or statistics ever could. Visiting a campus allows students to see themselves in a place, or not. That moment of connection, or lack of it, often tells the real story.

Finding Community and Balance

College is as much about learning how to live in a new world of independence, freedom, and responsibility as it is about academics. Students need spaces where they feel grounded.

For Jason, that came through music. At MIT, he joined the Logarhythms, an a cappella group that gave him joy and balance. After long hours in chemistry labs, singing with his group kept him sane. It went beyond just fun. It was vital for his mental health.

And he is not alone. Studies consistently show that students who get involved on campus, whether through clubs, mentoring, or activities, are more likely to stay in school and succeed. When students find their "Logarhythms," they build resilience, joy, and a sense of belonging.

Lessons in the Margins

- Financial aid opens doors, but persistence comes from feeling at home.

- Creativity and talents outside of academics can set a student apart.

- The steady habits built in high school matter more than a single test.

- Every student needs a place or a passion that keeps them grounded.

What Worked, What Didn't, and What Made All the Difference

What Worked

- Staying organized. Helping Jason track deadlines, polish applications, and showcase his music and art made the process manageable and memorable.

What Didn't

- Choosing schools based on brochures and websites alone. Some that looked ideal on paper didn't feel right in person; campus visits proved that fit mattered more than prestige.

What Made All the Difference

- Honoring Jason's identity, passions, and long-term goals. Selecting MIT gave him both academic challenge and a community where he truly belonged.

Strategies for Guiding High School Students Toward College

Strategy	Description	Example
Clarify goals early.	Encourage your teen to reflect on both personal values and academic aspirations when considering college paths.	Guide them in journaling about career dreams and identifying how different colleges align with those goals.
Research together.	Explore college programs, campus culture, and environments—not just rankings or prestige.	Create a side-by-side comparison chart of schools that match your teen's interests and strengths.
Stay on top of deadlines.	Break the college application and financial aid process into clear, manageable steps.	Use a shared family calendar to track forms, essay drafts, and scholarship due dates.
Prepare for costs.	Discuss financial realities early, including scholarships, grants, and budgeting habits.	Complete the FAFSA together and review all details before submission.
Encourage engagement.	Remind your teen that involvement beyond academics builds resilience and balance.	Support participation in clubs, volunteer work, or campus organizations that bring joy and confidence.

CHAPTER 14:
Preparing for Standardized Tests

*"Success is the sum of small efforts,
repeated day in and day out."*

—ROBERT COLLIER

If there's one phrase that can make a household tense, it's "Test day is coming." Over the years, as an educator, I've seen the sighs, the sharpened pencils, and the quiet anxiety that builds as the date approaches. For many students, standardized tests feel like mountains that have suddenly been placed in the middle of their path. And when something feels that big, children often carry the weight of it on their shoulders, with parents and caregivers feeling it right alongside them.

But here's the truth I want to share with parents and caregivers: These tests don't have to overwhelm us. With steady preparation, the right mindset, and some perspective, children can face them with confidence.

At home with Jason, test days were rarely dramatic. He was a disciplined, sit-still-and-highlight learner who annotated his notes and built steady routines. That discipline carried him far. Still, he wasn't untouched by the normal jitters of test-taking. Like many students, he sometimes needed reassurance that his preparation was enough and that one test could never define his future. What made the difference wasn't perfection but consistency. His habits provided a foundation, and the quiet encouragement reminded him that he didn't have to be flawless to do well.

Seeing Tests for What They Are and What They Aren't

As parents and caregivers, we know standardized tests matter. They can influence class placements, scholarships, and even college admissions. But they don't define a child's worth or tell the whole story of who they are. Research shows test scores often say more about access to tutors, quiet study spaces, and resources than about true ability.

I reminded Jason the same way I reminded my students: "This test is important, but it doesn't get to decide your value. You are more than a number on a page."

That perspective eased Jason's occasional nerves and kept the focus on what he could control: preparation, effort, and mindset.

The Uneven Playing Field

Standardized tests are often written with a narrow frame of reference, and that can quietly disadvantage students. A reading passage about lacrosse might confuse a child who has never seen the sport. A math word problem framed around sailing may be second nature to one child but foreign to another. The content itself is not the issue, but the cultural assumptions built into the questions that create gaps before the test-taker even begins to solve the problem.

In classrooms, I saw this regularly. Students who were bright and capable hesitated, not because they lacked skill but because the question itself introduced unfamiliar ground. Imagine a student who has mastered fractions but stumbles over a test problem about dividing opera tickets, simply because they have never encountered that word before. In those moments, the test becomes less about knowledge and more about exposure.

Parents and caregivers can bridge this gap by:

- Encouraging children to read from a wide range of sources, from science articles to travel pieces.
- Talking about new vocabulary words encountered in books, shows, or conversations.
- Using everyday activities as learning moments. Cooking can become a math lesson, and a sports game can teach strategy and statistics.

For children learning English or managing learning differences, advocacy is crucial. Accommodations such as extra time, small-group settings, or technology aids are not advantages; they are lifelines. Caregivers who speak up help ensure the playing field is as fair as possible.

The goal isn't to master opera or lacrosse. The goal is to prepare children to face the unfamiliar with confidence rather than fear.

Finding the Study Rhythm That Fits

One mistake I've seen parents and caregivers make is assuming studying must look one way: quiet, still, and rigid. That works for some children, but for others it feels like trying to fit into shoes that don't belong to them.

Jason was comfortable with traditional study methods. His discipline gave him structure, but even so, he sometimes needed a short break to reset or a reminder to trust the work he had already done. His study rhythm worked because it was consistent and realistic for him.

Other students I taught needed very different approaches:

- **Visual Learners:** These individuals tend to remember information best when it is presented in diagrams, charts, or color-coded notes. One student turned every science unit into a poster of images and arrows, and it stuck far better than flashcards.

- **Auditory Learners:** Some children thrive when they record themselves reading notes and replay them like music. Others benefit from reading aloud to a parent or sibling.

- **Kinesthetic Learners:** For some, sitting still is the enemy of retention. These students do better walking around the room with flashcards, acting out historical events, or clapping rhythms while memorizing facts.

- **Reading/Writing Learners:** These students do well with outlines, summaries, and written reflections. Jason fit neatly here, as his annotations became a map for his memory.

The best gift we can give children is permission to study in a way that fits them rather than what fits our expectations. A child who does well while pacing with vocabulary words is no less serious than one who sits quietly highlighting. Both are learning, just differently.

Practice tests can also be powerful. Although Jason was a strong student, he still benefited from reviewing test formats occasionally. For my students, practice didn't always bring confidence, but it did bring familiarity. Seeing the structure ahead of time removed some of the mystery and made the test feel a little less intimidating. For parents, the key is to frame practice not as judgment but as rehearsal. It is also a chance to notice where time slips away, where comprehension holds steady, and what minor adjustments might help next time.

When Nerves Get Loud

Even the most disciplined students can feel butterflies on test day. Jason was no exception. Before a big exam, he sometimes admitted, "I feel a little shaky." We would discuss ways to steady himself, such as reviewing what he knew, breathing deeply, and remembering that one test could not define him.

For many of my students, nerves were not something that disappeared, but something that had to be managed. The goal was not perfect calm, but enough steadiness to move forward. Students can try simple tools to keep going when anxiety shows up:

- **Breathing on Purpose:** Inhale for four counts, hold for two, exhale for six. Repeat until the body begins to settle.
- **Grounding:** Look around and name five things you see, four things you hear, three you can touch, two you can smell, and one you can taste.

- **Performing Dress Rehearsals:** Create practice conditions at home by setting up a quiet space, using timed sections, and taking short breaks, so the test environment feels more familiar.

Encouragement also plays a role. A few reassuring words before leaving for school, or even helping children practice quiet affirmations in their minds, can remind them that they are prepared and capable. These small strategies don't erase anxiety, but they give students tools to keep moving through it.

The Bigger Picture

Tests matter, but they're not everything. They don't measure creativity, kindness, or resilience. They don't capture the determination it takes to keep trying when life gets tough.

And not every student's path includes college, and that's more than okay. Skilled trades such as plumbing, electrical work, HVAC, and auto repair require intelligence, discipline, and specialized training. They keep communities running.

What matters most is that children see a path forward that aligns with their unique talents and abilities. For some, standardized tests are part of that path. For others, vocational certifications or apprenticeships provide a pathway. All are worthy. All are necessary.

Lessons in the Margins

- Encourage your child to start early, but to keep study time light. Two twenty-minute sessions a day are more effective than a five-hour cram.

- Prompt your child to review both the content and the test format. Familiarity lowers fear and builds confidence.

- Prioritize rest, nourishment, and laughter. A well-cared for body supports a focused mind.

- Request testing or classroom accommodations in writing and follow up accordingly. Fairness often requires advocacy.

- Celebrate effort, not just results. Recognizing small steps forward reinforces persistence and self-belief.

- If the material goes beyond what you can comfortably teach, shift your role from instructor to guide. Help your child find the right resources—a tutor, online videos, a peer study group, or extra help from a teacher. What matters most is not having all the answers but showing your child that learning is a lifelong pursuit worth investing in.

What Worked, What Didn't, What Made All the Difference

What Worked
- Building steady routines, reviewing test formats, and matching study methods to Jason's strengths.

What Didn't
- Cramming, late nights, or treating tests as the ultimate verdict.

What Made all the Difference
- Keeping perspective. Jason knew he was loved and supported, even when he felt nervous or made mistakes.
- That steady reassurance helped him face tests with calm and confidence.

Strategies to Prepare for Standardized Tests

Strategy	Description	Example
Understand the format.	Review the test structure, timing, and question types together so your child feels confident and prepared.	Go over a sample test to determine whether it includes multiple-choice, essays, or short-answer questions.
Make a realistic plan.	Help your child build a steady, balanced study schedule that fits their energy and daily routines.	Set aside short sessions on different days. For example, math on Mondays and reading on Tuesdays to prevent burnout.
Practice and reflect.	Encourage your child to take practice tests and go over what worked well and what can be improved.	Ask, "What felt easy? What do you want to work on next time?" after each practice round.
Teach test-smart moves.	Model strategies that make testing more manageable, such as pacing, prioritizing, and staying calm under pressure.	Remind your child it's okay to skip a tough question and return to it later.
Calm the nerves.	Create a soothing pre-test routine to manage anxiety and boost confidence.	Practice deep breathing together or share a positive affirmation before test day.

CHAPTER 15:

Discussing Identity and Civic Responsibility

"Our lives begin to end the day we become silent about things that matter."

—MARTIN LUTHER KING JR.

Discussing Identity in a Social and Cultural Context

Understanding one's identity is not a single moment but a lifelong journey. From the time children first ask questions like, "Why does my skin look different?" or "Where did our family come from?" they begin to piece together who they are. Identity is shaped at home first through heritage, culture, faith, and traditions, and it continues to grow as children interact with school, peers, and the larger world.

As parents and caregivers, we are our children's first teachers in this area. Sharing heritage, telling family stories, and teaching values help children understand their roots. Books, films, and community events that reflect a child's cultural background can strengthen that understanding, but identity does not stop with ancestry. It is also influenced by the community to which they belong, the responsibilities they carry, and the way society perceives and shapes them.

For our family, this connection between identity and civic responsibility was never abstract. It was lived out in real time. We made a point to share with Jason both the joys and the hardships of our journey, because we wanted him to understand not only who he was but also the responsibility that comes with belonging to something bigger than himself.

Our Family's Journey

My husband and I are deeply tied to our Antiguan roots, but our story expanded when we became part of the American story. Allison's path took him through the United States Navy, where he served with honor during some of the most challenging moments of the 1980s. His deployment to Grenada during the invasion and later his assignment in Lebanon during the October 1983 bombing that took the lives of over 200 marines marked him forever. Those experiences were not just military service. They were lessons in courage, sacrifice, and the sobering reality of what it means to serve a country.

My journey looked very different. I came to America at the age of twenty and began working as a live-in housekeeper. The days were long, filled with caring for children and maintaining households. It was humbling work, but it built in me a resilience that carried me forward. Over time, I transitioned into office jobs, including over eight years as a secretary at the Board of Jewish Education, more than eight years as a communications coordinator at Time Warner, and a little over four years as a secretary in the Department of Biochemistry at Stony Brook University. During this period, I also began attending college part-time. All of these experiences came before I was accepted as a Teaching Fellow and started my career as a special education teacher in the New York City public school system. Teaching in underserved communities was not easy, but it was where I felt most alive, empowering students who had been told in subtle and not-so-subtle ways that they were less capable than others.

Together, our stories, his years of service in the Navy, followed by more than three decades with New York City Transit, and my years working as a secretary before entering the classroom, were the foundation we wanted Jason to see clearly. They were not stories to polish or hide. They were real accounts of hardship, steady work, growth, and service that connected him both to the Caribbean heritage we carried and to the American dream we had worked so hard to claim.

By drawing these connections, Jason could see how identity is not static. It grows with each generation, influenced by both history and choice. We wanted him to know that identity is never just a personal matter. It is also communal, woven into the larger cultural fabric.

Civic Responsibility as a Daily Practice

For many people, civic responsibility is only evident in moments of voting, protests, or speeches. But we taught Jason that it begins much earlier, in the everyday decisions we make:

- Returning a lost wallet instead of keeping it.
- Respecting others even when opinions differ.
- Picking up trash in a shared space.
- Volunteering to help at a school event.

These may seem small, but they are the building blocks of citizenship. A child who learns to care for their community in these everyday ways is more likely to step into bigger responsibilities later with confidence and conviction.

We often reminded Jason that being part of a society is not about what you can take from it, but what you contribute. It is about asking: "What kind of neighbor, student, and friend will I be?"

Encouraging Political Awareness and Activism

As Jason grew older, his questions grew bigger. He wanted to know about fairness, about laws, about justice. These were not simple questions, and we did not always have simple answers. But we leaned into the conversations anyway, because silence teaches children more than we realize. Silence can suggest indifference. And indifference is not what we wanted him to inherit.

We encouraged him to read about issues that mattered, to listen to perspectives different from his own, and to recognize that activism comes in many forms. Sometimes it is marching in a peaceful protest. At other times, it may involve signing an online petition, volunteering at a food pantry, or mentoring a younger child. The important thing is not the size of the act but the willingness to act.

We told him: "Your voice matters. Never think you are too small to make a difference."

Addressing Bias and Profiling

Of all the conversations we had, the most challenging were those about bias and profiling. They were difficult because they were real.

We had to prepare Jason not for the world as it should be but for the world as it is. That meant sitting him down and discussing what to do if a police officer ever stopped him. We role-played scenarios, reminding him to stay calm, keep his hands visible, and speak respectfully. These were not lessons any parent wishes to give, but they were necessary.

Hearing Jason later describe times when officers had stopped him was both heartbreaking and strangely reassuring. Heartbreaking because no young man should have to live with that reality. Reassuring because the lessons we had drilled into him helped keep him safe.

Bias and discrimination are still very much alive, but by talking openly about them, we equipped Jason with both awareness and resilience. We gave him tools not just to survive but to stand tall in his identity and his dignity.

Family Discussions on Rights and Responsibilities

Identity and civic responsibility are not one-time talks. They are ongoing conversations. Families can create safe spaces where children are free to ask questions, express their opinions, and explore ideas.

Sometimes that meant watching a movie together and then asking reflective questions:

- "What would you have done differently if you were the main character?"
- "How did their identity shape the choices they made?"

Books became another doorway:

- *The Name Jar* by Yangsook Choi opened conversations about fitting in and belonging.
- *To Kill a Mockingbird* by Harper Lee helped us explore the themes of justice, prejudice, and moral courage.

- *Night* by Elie Wiesel deepened our understanding of resilience, humanity, and the importance of remembering history.

And sometimes it was community service, like visiting nursing homes and singing for the residents, that made the lessons come alive. These were not abstract ideals but lived practices of rights and responsibilities.

By combining stories, books, films, service, and everyday talks, Jason learned that his identity is not only about who he is, but about how he chooses to show up for others.

Lessons in the Margins

- Identity is shaped by both our origins and the way we choose to live in community.

- Children watch us closely. Our actions speak louder than our words when it comes to civic responsibility.

- Conversations about bias and injustice may be painful, but they are essential for survival and dignity.

- Activism begins with awareness and grows through small, consistent acts of responsibility.

- The goal is not to raise children who simply "fit in," but to raise children who know who they are and how to contribute with courage.

What Worked, What Didn't, and What Made All the Difference

What Worked

- Sharing our family's personal stories, my husband's service, and my immigrant journey, helping Jason see identity not as abstract but as real and lived.

- Using books, movies, and community service to make significant concepts understandable and practical.

What Didn't

- Trying to shield Jason from the realities of racial profiling by softening or postponing the truth.

- My hesitation, though protective, left him less prepared when those realities appeared. Balancing honesty with innocence was a constant struggle.

What Made All the Difference

- Making identity, rights, and responsibility part of everyday conversation—not "special occasion talks."

- These steady, honest exchanges built resilience instead of fear and helped Jason see himself as both grounded in identity and committed to social responsibility.

Strategies for Discussing Identity and Civic Responsibility

Strategy	Description	Example
Share family stories.	Talk about your family's heritage, struggles, and contributions so your child understands how identity connects to responsibility.	Share an ancestor's immigration or resilience story and link it to your family's role in today's community.
Model everyday civic acts.	Demonstrate responsibility through daily choices rooted in kindness, fairness, and service.	Take your child with you to vote, volunteer, or participate in a community cleanup.
Encourage activism.	Support your child's interest in causes that matter to them and teach that their voice can create change.	Help your child join a local campaign, club, or awareness project at school.
Role-play bias situations.	Prepare your child to navigate uncomfortable discriminatory encounters safely and confidently.	Practice what to do if approached unfairly or questioned by authority figures.
Use books and media.	Select stories and films that spark meaningful conversations about identity, fairness and belonging.	Discuss *The Name Jar* and reflect together on what it teaches about respect and inclusion.

CHAPTER 16:

Building Financial Literacy

*"The number one problem in today's generation
and economy is the lack of financial literacy."*

—ALAN GREENSPAN

Lessons I Wish We'd Taught Early

Financial independence doesn't appear overnight when a child turns
eighteen. It grows out of daily habits, small choices, and early conversations. Looking back, I realize there were lessons I wish we had
taught Jason much earlier and more intentionally.

We didn't create allowances or set up "Save, Spend, and Give" jars
like many parents do. We didn't use spreadsheets or budgeting charts
as teaching tools. Instead, Jason mainly learned by watching us. Allison
and I lived simply. We avoided unnecessary debt, resisted chasing after
trends, and made the most of what we had. That was our classroom.

Those lessons in frugality had a profound impact on Jason. He saw that you don't buy what you can't afford, that needs come before wants, and that saving for the future brings peace of mind. Without us ever calling it a "lesson," he absorbed the idea that money is something to manage with care.

Still, I know there were gaps. I wish we had started those money conversations earlier, about saving but also about credit, debt, and even small-scale entrepreneurship. Jason grew into financial wisdom, but some of his learning came later than it could have. In hindsight, it reminds me that while modeling is powerful, children benefit when we pair example with conversation.

Navigating Big Financial Milestones

Facing Student Loans and Financial Aid

By the time Jason was preparing for college, the "money talk" became unavoidable. Higher education brought financial realities that couldn't be ignored: scholarships, financial aid, and the possibility of student loans.

We did not have long conversations about interest rates or repayment plans because Jason was awarded two full scholarships. One was to the University of Pittsburgh, where they wanted to recruit him into their mathematics program. The other was to Brandeis, which would have covered everything except the cost of books. From an early age, he had been raised to believe that he would go to college on scholarships, and he made that vision a reality through hard work and consistency.

Still, Jason had his own preferences. He was drawn to Boston College because of its beautiful surroundings—the architecture, the tree-lined paths, the overall sense of calm. But the financial package there wasn't generous enough. MIT, on the other hand, offered a grant-based package that made far more sense for our family, even though it didn't cover every expense. We encouraged him to consider that offer, knowing it would allow him to study without placing too heavy a financial burden on us.

Ultimately, Jason determined that the environments at the University of Pittsburgh and Brandeis were not the right fit for him, and we decided it was best not to force him to accept those scholarships. What mattered most was that he had choices.

Learning About Credit and Planning Ahead

Credit awareness came next. For Jason, the idea of borrowing money and having to repay it was no surprise. He had seen us avoid debt unless it was necessary. But credit scores and the invisible weight they carry were new concepts.

At first, credit seemed abstract to him. Why would a number matter so much? But as we tied it to milestones—buying a car, renting an apartment, owning a home—he understood. Poor credit wasn't just a set of numbers on paper; it was a barrier to independence. Good credit wasn't about prestige; it was about freedom.

This is an area I regret. I didn't emphasize it strongly or early enough, though thankfully, Jason has never been a big spender. Even so, I realized too late that teaching about credit is as essential as teaching about saving.

We also introduced him to the basics of financial planning: setting aside emergency savings, understanding how retirement funds grow, and learning that investing isn't only for the wealthy. Even if some of these concepts felt far off, Jason listened. He respected the wisdom because he saw how much smoother life became when money didn't control us.

Expanding the Vision: Beyond Survival Toward Stewardship

Myra's Guidance: Family Wisdom as a Legacy

One of the best decisions we made was to involve my sister, Myra, in Jason's financial education. With her degree in financial management, she had both expertise and a practical approach that Jason respected. She taught him about saving for retirement early, how to evaluate investments, and how to think of money as a tool rather than a burden.

What Jason gained from her wasn't just information; it was vision. Myra helped him see that financial planning wasn't about fear or scarcity, but about stewardship and growth. Her mentorship underscored something important: Financial literacy can be passed down not only by parents but also by family members who possess expertise and a willingness to share it.

Her influence made me realize that even if I didn't teach every lesson directly, I had still given Jason the most essential piece: the right models. Myra's knowledge was built on the foundation of frugality that he had already observed at home.

Entrepreneurship: The Lesson Still Unfolding

If there is one area that continues to unfold for me, it is entrepreneurship. Jason grew up financially careful, but I didn't always encourage him enough to explore creating something of his own. My own entrepreneurial journey began later through making hot sauces, crocheting, and now, writing. I haven't yet earned from my writing, but I am building toward that goal with hope and intention, trusting that it will one day provide both income and legacy.

That journey has already taught me valuable lessons. Far beyond profit, entrepreneurship is about daring to create, using your gifts to serve others, and discovering new possibilities for freedom. The process itself fosters resilience, confidence, and a clear vision.

Parents and caregivers can give children this perspective much earlier. Small projects, such as a lemonade stand, bake sale, or craft sale, can teach valuable lessons in profit and loss, customer service, and perseverance. More importantly, they show children that they can use their creativity to build something meaningful.

When children see that they can create value and generate income, even in simple ways, money shifts from being something to manage for survival to being a tool for building, serving, and dreaming. That shift can change their entire relationship with financial responsibility.

Lessons in the Margins

- Children learn as much from what we model as from what we teach.

- Frugality and simplicity can be a classroom without words.

- Honest conversations about loans, credit, and planning are never too late, but the sooner the better.

- Family expertise is a gift—share it across generations.

- Entrepreneurship transforms money lessons from survival to creativity and vision.

What Worked, What Didn't, and What Made All the Difference

What Worked

- Modeling simple living and avoiding unnecessary debt gave Jason a quiet but powerful foundation.

- He learned to see money not as something to spend quickly but as something to manage wisely.

What Didn't

- Waiting too long to discuss credit and entrepreneurship intentionally.

- By the time we did, Jason was ready to act independently, but those lessons could have had an even stronger impact if introduced earlier.

What Made All the Difference

- Letting Jason learn through observation and through Myra's mentorship.

- Together, they shaped his financial awareness into more than responsibility; they helped it grow into financial wisdom.

Strategies for Teaching Financial Responsibility and Management

Strategy	Description	Example
Model simplicity and frugality.	Show your child how to prioritize needs over wants.	Talk through your own decisions: "We'll wait to buy that because it's not a need."
Practice hands-on money management.	Let your child handle real money to build responsibility.	Allow children a weekly allowance and encourage them to save part of it.
Open a savings account together.	Teach the value of interest, security, and saving for goals.	Open a youth savings account and celebrate progress as their balance grows.
Discuss credit and debt honestly.	Prepare teens for real-world borrowing and its consequences.	Use examples of credit card interest to illustrate how debt can grow if left unmanaged.
Introduce entrepreneurship early.	Encourage small ventures that build independence and innovation.	Support a bake sale or craft project, guiding your child through profit and customer care.

CHAPTER 17:

Health and Wellness

"Take care of your body. It's the
only place you have to live."

—JIM ROHN

The Overlooked Partner in Learning

Health and wellness weren't something I set out to teach Jason directly. I wasn't drawing up nutrition charts or enrolling him in elaborate exercise programs. Honestly, I didn't think of myself as "teaching health" at all. However, what I did do was cook most of our meals at home, ensure he got rest, and model a life that wasn't about overspending or overindulging.

Without realizing it, those simple habits of moderation and routine became Jason's first lessons in wellness. And those lessons, I've come to see, matter just as much as homework or grades.

Children cannot perform well in the classroom if their bodies are exhausted, their emotions are bottled up, or their minds are racing with stress. Health isn't a side note to education. It is part of the foundation.

Physical Health: A Steady Anchor

If I could do it again, I would put even more energy into physical health. Children need nutritious food, regular physical activity, and adequate sleep. Those are the anchors that steady them.

Homegrown and Home-Cooked

In our backyard, we grew callaloo, eggplants, zucchini, butternut squash, okra, and cucumbers. In the summer months, my kitchen was filled with fresh greens and vegetables that went straight from the soil to the table. Jason may not have realized it at the time, but he was learning something important: Food could be simple, fresh, and nourishing.

Of course, there were times when he had fast food like any other child. But home-cooked meals were always the priority. A pot of rice and peas, baked fish, sautéed callaloo, or soup packed with vegetables was the norm. Looking back, I see how grounding those meals were. They were about nourishing the soul as much as the belly. They shaped energy levels, concentration, and long-term health.

Parents and caregivers sometimes underestimate the power of the everyday meal. You don't need expensive ingredients or complicated recipes. Even a pot of rice paired with greens can provide a foundation of wellness that children will carry with them long after they leave the table.

Tennis and Movement

For Jason, tennis became his steady outlet from middle school onward. Tennis wasn't just about championships or trophies. The game itself focused on regular practice, body movement, and developing coordination and stamina.

Tennis taught him discipline. He showed up for lessons, drills, and matches, even on the hottest days, while balancing his athletic commitments with school responsibilities. On some afternoons, he went straight from the classroom to the court, and on others, he managed practice after finishing his assignments. Tennis gave him a sense of belonging. On the court, he was not just a student, but a student-athlete learning the value of persistence.

But here's the difficult part of the story. Over time, Jason's enthusiasm for tennis began to fade. The emphasis on improvement and performance gradually outweighed the fun of simply playing. What once gave him energy and balance started to feel more like work than joy.

This experience reminded me of an important lesson as a parent. Encouragement fuels growth, but joy must remain part of the process. When tennis began to feel more like pressure than play, I realized that effort alone is not enough if the spark of enjoyment is lost. Children need guidance, yes, and they also need permission to listen to their own feelings. My role was not to push him harder, but to help him rediscover balance. To remember why he started, and to know that walking away would not mean failure. True growth happens when children learn to honor both their discipline and their delight.

Key Insights

- Keep meals nourishing but straightforward. Home cooking, even when basic, is powerful.
- Encourage one physical activity your child enjoys. The activity matters less than the consistency.
- Praise effort more than results. Support builds resilience, while constant criticism erodes joy.
- Protect bedtime. A well-rested child learns better than one who burns out.

Mental Health: Opening the Door We Once Kept Closed

When I was growing up, we didn't talk about mental health. You just pressed on. But silence doesn't erase feelings. It only buries them.

As Jason grew older, I saw the strain of balancing academics, activities, and expectations. Initially, I didn't have the correct language to address it. Over time, I learned that even small conversations mattered: asking how he was feeling, pausing together to breathe, or simply admitting, "This is a lot right now."

Those conversations opened a door for him that had stayed closed in my own childhood. They showed him emotions weren't a weakness. They were signals.

And here's what I learned as a teacher: Children carry unspoken burdens into the classroom. I recall a student who would come to school exhausted every day. When I asked why, she told me her mother had friends over late into the night, and since she slept in the living room, she barely got any rest. That student taught me something I've seen over and over again: academic performance and emotional well-being are deeply connected.

Key Insights

- Make emotions part of everyday conversations. A quick "How are you feeling?" goes further than silence.
- Recognize that behavior is communication. A withdrawn child may not be "defiant." They may be overwhelmed.
- Encourage open dialogue about emotions. Even if you stumble over words, starting the conversation matters.

Stress Management: Learning to Pause

Stress will always be part of life. The key isn't to eliminate it but to manage it.

As a parent, I encouraged Jason to take breaks, but as a teacher, I also saw the cost when children weren't given space to reset. That's why I introduced brain breaks in my classroom. Short moments for stretching, breathing, or moving around. These brain breaks were incredibly effective in improving focus. But not everyone understood these pauses. I was reprimanded once because an administrator thought I was wasting instructional time. The truth is, those "wasted" minutes were often the most productive in the long run.

Parents and caregivers sometimes believe that the more a child studies, the better the results will be. But too much pressure can backfire. Breaks, balance, and coping strategies make studying more effective.

Key Insights

- Teach short, simple stress-relief techniques, such as breathing exercises or taking a walk outside, before a test.
- Don't equate longer hours with better learning. Smart studying beats endless studying.

- Build stress management into daily routines. Pausing is not laziness. It is wisdom.

Medical Check-Ups: Building Comfort with Care

Doctor visits can feel intimidating for children. I didn't want Jason to see them that way, so we treated them as if they were routine. He had the same pediatrician for about nine years, which helped build trust. The doctor explained things clearly, and Jason, who was fascinated by medicine for a time, asked his own questions.

Consistency of care matters. When children see the same doctor, dentist, or nurse over time, they build confidence in the process. Parents and caregivers can help by explaining what will happen at each visit and modeling calmness.

Key Insights

- Present check-ups as ordinary, not frightening. Explain each step in simple terms.
- Encourage children to pay attention to their bodies and speak up if something feels uncomfortable or wrong.
- Treat healthcare as a partnership, not a punishment.

Lessons in the Margins

- A home-cooked meal can anchor a child's health more than any nutrition chart.
- Silence around mental health is a barrier. Break it, even imperfectly.
- Wellness doesn't require perfection. It requires consistency.
- Encouragement fuels growth. Overcriticism stifles it.

What Worked, What Didn't, What Made All the Difference

What Worked

- Incorporating consistent exercise. Jason's regular exercise through tennis gave him balance, focus, and resilience without us needing to call it "fitness."

What Didn't

- Overlooking stress management in the early years.
- Our focus on academics sometimes overshadowed balance, leaving Jason to learn coping tools later than he should have.

What Made All the Difference

- Creating an open home where emotions were welcomed, not hidden.

- Once we began talking honestly about stress and feelings, Jason grew stronger in ways grades could never measure.

Strategies for Weaving Health into Daily Life

Strategy	Description	Example
Promote physical activity.	Encourage regular movement in fun, sustainable ways.	Play tennis, take family walks, or dance together at home.
Prioritize nutrition.	Serve balanced meals that fit your family's culture and routine.	Include rice, peas, callaloo, fish, soups, and fresh vegetables.
Foster mental health awareness.	Make emotions part of daily conversation.	Share "highs and lows" at dinner, journal, or practice mindfulness.
Model stress management.	Teach coping tools early and normalize rest.	Practice deep breathing while in traffic or take short breaks between work calls.
Protect healthy sleep habits.	Treat bedtime as essential for growth and focus.	Keep a steady sleep schedule, avoid screens, and create a calm evening routine.

CHAPTER 18:

The Journey Beyond College

"If you can dream it, you can do it."

—WALT DISNEY

Entering the World Beyond College: A New Chapter Begins

There is something unforgettable about watching students throw their caps into the air at graduation. For a few seconds, time seems suspended. Dreams hang in the balance alongside those flying tassels. Behind each cap is a story: years of classes, late nights, missed family gatherings, friendships, heartbreaks, and triumphs.

As parents and caregivers, we often imagine that the day our children graduate from college will mark the end of a long journey. In reality, graduation is another beginning. For Jason, it was not the end of his educational journey but the start of a new season. He did not immediately step into the workforce. Instead, he had already set his sights on graduate school. His heart was drawn toward ministry, service, and scholarship. That calling led him to Duke University, where he enrolled in a Master of Divinity program.

I remember the mix of pride and relief I felt at his college graduation. The long hours of study, the financial sacrifices, and the encouragement during difficult times had all led to that moment. What I did not anticipate was how quickly the questions would shift. "What's next?" became the constant refrain. Jason's answer was clear: more preparation, more growth, and more learning before stepping into a full-time role.

The transition from college into the next stage of life carries both excitement and uncertainty. Some young adults choose jobs, others pursue graduate or professional school, and still others take time to explore. Regardless of the choice, each graduate is stepping into unknown territory. At this stage, parents, caregivers and mentors remain vital. We may not be able to take the tests or write the papers, but we can steady our children as they find their footing in adulthood.

Key Insights

- Discuss the transition openly with your child in advance of graduation. Ask, "What do you imagine life looking like in the first year after college?"
- Help them frame their next steps not as permanent decisions but as part of a continuing journey of growth.

Career Planning: Education as Foundation

The transition from college to graduate study or professional life is one of the most significant milestones a young adult will face. It is not just about academic preparation, but also about clarifying one's values, passions, and direction.

Jason's choice to pursue divinity at Duke meant that his preparation was both intellectual and deeply personal. He wanted to combine study with service, faith with action. Later, he continued his studies at Duke, pursuing a Master of Theology, where he delved deeper into questions of calling and purpose. At the same time, he worked as a lab technician in epidemiology, balancing scientific research with his graduate studies. He also spent time as an admissions counselor at North Carolina Central University, guiding students as they charted their own futures.

From the outside, these roles might have appeared to be distractions from his larger goals. In reality, they were essential parts of his preparation. Each role provided him with perspective, broadened his skills, and added practical experience to complement his academic growth.

Key Insights

- Encourage your children to view graduate studies, internships, or early jobs as stepping stones to their future goals.
- Ask them, "What skills or insights are you gaining from this experience?"
- Help them connect the dots between today's experiences and tomorrow's opportunities.

The Power of Networking and Mentorship

Education can get a young adult to the table, but relationships often help them stay there.

Mentorship played a critical role in Jason's journey. His warm and engaging spirit opened doors to people who guided him during seasons of uncertainty. When he weighed graduate school options, it was a mentor who helped him think beyond school rankings and reputation to consider where he would thrive as a whole person.

In our Caribbean heritage, elders have always played a vital role. "Aunties" and "uncles," whether by blood or by bond, often stepped in with wisdom and guidance. Mentors in professional and academic spaces serve a similar purpose. They are the ones who have walked ahead and are willing to share their light with those who follow.

Networking also proved decisive for Jason. Through alum connections and platforms like LinkedIn, he did more than collect contacts. He asked thoughtful questions, engaged with people's work, and built genuine relationships. Those connections shaped opportunities he might not have discovered otherwise. His mentors and networks together became anchors when he doubted himself and encouragement when he needed direction.

Key Insights

- Normalize mentorship.
- Share stories of mentors who influenced your life, and encourage your children to seek out guides who will challenge and support them.
- Teach them that networking is not about collecting business cards or digital contacts but about building authentic, long-term relationships.

Preparing for a Career and Calling

Jason's path illustrates that building a career is rarely a straightforward process. Graduate school, part-time work, admissions counseling, and laboratory research all contributed to shaping his story. None of these experiences were wasted. Every step added tenacity, perspective, and growth.

Practical preparation matters just as much as vision. Résumés, cover letters, and interview skills may seem basic, but they often determine whether opportunities open or close. Early in Jason's journey, we underestimated the importance of preparing résumés and interview skills before applications were due. While we encouraged him to dream big, we did not emphasize those technical details soon enough. As a result, he had to learn quickly under pressure. It became a valuable growth opportunity, but one that could have been smoother with earlier preparation.

Soft skills also matter. Communicating with colleagues, managing expectations, and navigating workplace dynamics are essential. These lessons are not always taught in classrooms but are often modeled at home and in community life. The way we treat neighbors, collaborate in spiritual communities or civic groups, or resolve family disagreements gives our children unspoken lessons they carry into professional spaces.

Key Insights

- Begin teaching practical preparation early.
- Encourage your child to keep a "living résumé" that they update regularly.
- Model professional skills in your own interactions, and talk openly about challenges and solutions you face in your workplace or community.

Embracing Change and Building a Life

The journey beyond college is not about rushing into the work-force. It is about building a meaningful path. For Jason, that meant completing graduate studies before stepping into a full-time role. For other young adults, it may look different. What matters is reminding our children that they already carry the tools, values, and resilience to navigate whatever comes next.

As parents and caregivers, our role shifts but never disappears. We move from directors to encouragers. We may not call the plays anymore, but our voices of support still matter. We remind our children that it is normal to stumble, to change direction, and to discover new passions along the way.

Education never truly ends. It simply moves into new spaces: classrooms, workplaces, ministries, laboratories, and communities. Our responsibility is to continue encouraging our children to grow into the fullness of their purpose.

Lessons in the Margins

- Success beyond college is not about perfection. Success is about persistence.

- Mentorship and networking are lifelines that provide wisdom, direction, and opportunities.

- Networking is most effective when it is rooted in genuine curiosity and authentic connection.

- Soft skills, such as communication and adaptability, often matter as much as technical skills.

- Parents remain guides even when their role changes from directing to encouraging.

What Worked, What Didn't, and What Made All the Difference

What Worked

- Making the most of mentorship and networking, which expanded Jason's opportunities and helped him align his choices with his calling.

What Didn't

- Underestimating the importance of preparing résumés and interview skills early. Waiting until the last minute created unnecessary pressure.

What Made All the Difference

- Cultivating mentors and networks that offered both professional guidance and emotional support.

- Those relationships grounded Jason through seasons of uncertainty and change.

Strategies for Parents, Caregivers, and Educators

Strategy	Why It Matters	How to Put It into Practice
Explore graduate and career paths early.	Helps your child see beyond short-term goals and plan intentionally for the future.	Discuss long-term aspirations early and expose them to possibilities.
Model soft skills.	Highlights how communication, collaboration, and adaptability shape academic and career success.	Demonstrate teamwork, practice conflict resolution and collaboration, and show adaptability in action.
Normalize mentorship and networking.	Provides guidance, accountability, and access to valuable opportunities.	Share your own mentorship stories and encourage your child to seek guidance and trusted adults.
Introduce networking platforms.	Builds digital connections and strengthens career readiness.	Help your child create a LinkedIn profile and model authentic professional engagement.
Reframe setbacks.	Shows that failure is part of growth and resilience.	Remind your child that detours often lead to discovery and personal strength.

CHAPTER 19:
Conclusion — Invest in Your Children

"Children are not a distraction from more important work. They are the most critical work."

—DR. JOHN TRAINER, MD

The Heart of Raising a Scholar

When I look back over the years of raising Jason, I realize that raising a scholar is about much more than ensuring high grades or preparing for exams. It is about shaping a whole person: curious, compassionate, thoughtful, and ready to take their place in the world.

Yes, academics matter. A child's ability to read deeply, write clearly, and think critically will serve them in every stage of life. But scholars are not created by textbooks alone. Kitchen-table conversations, the questions they dare to ask, the communities that nurture them, and the resilience they build when life pushes hard shape them.

To raise a well-rounded scholar is to encourage curiosity alongside discipline, imagination alongside structure, and courage alongside caution. It is to nurture the intellectual life, yes, but also the emotional and social lives that will shape how a child navigates the world. *Scholars are raised, not left to chance.*

For Jason, raising a scholar meant excelling in school while also finding outlets for his passions in church, community service, and friendships that stretched his perspective. It meant learning to carry both the weight of expectations and the joy of discovery. And for us, as his parents, it meant repeatedly choosing to prioritize his growth over our own fleeting pleasures.

The Broader Societal Implications

When we invest in our children, we are not just shaping individuals. We are shaping the future of our communities and society. A child who develops both intellectual skill and compassion becomes a leader capable of uniting logic with empathy. A young person who understands both science and social justice can solve problems that demand both innovation and compassion.

Education, when done well, is never only personal. It ripples outward. Well-rounded scholars grow into adults who enrich our workplaces, strengthen our neighborhoods, and challenge injustices wherever they see them. They remind us that learning finds its true purpose when knowledge is applied in service of something greater. **Because education has such a wide ripple effect, diversity, inclusion, and social justice matter deeply in every classroom.**

These elements are not extras; they are essential if we want to raise leaders who can stand in the complexity of today's world. When education affirms every child's dignity and potential, it lays the foundation for a more equitable society.

Jason's academic path is one example of what educational investment looks like in practice:

- Honor roll student throughout elementary, middle, and high school.
- MIT graduate with a degree in chemistry.
- Two master's degrees in divinity and theology from Duke University.
- A master's degree in human services and psychology and a PhD in community psychology from the University of Maryland, Baltimore County.

More important than the degrees are the ways Jason is utilizing them—to conduct research, to teach, to initiate conversations about racial injustice, and to make a positive impact on people's lives. His journey is not just about his success; it's about his life. It is about the possibility of what happens when a child's capacity is seen, nurtured, and supported by family, educators, and community.

Reflections on Our Journey

Raising a young Black man in America has been a journey filled with both triumphs and trials. There were nights when Allison and I lay awake, worrying whether our son's teachers would see his brilliance or allow their biases to cloud his grades. There were meetings with administrators where we insisted that fairness, not favoritism, guide his teachers' decisions.

I still remember one high school conversation with Jason after a teacher's comment left him discouraged. I told him, "Do not let a single comment stop you. Someone else's perception does not determine your worth." His father added, "We will keep standing with you." Those words were not grand speeches; they were lifelines, moments when Jason knew we had his back.

Most of Jason's teachers were supportive and caring, and for that support, we remain deeply grateful. However, the advocacy we were required to provide in a few challenging moments revealed something important—children reach their full potential when adults refuse to be silent.

That lesson carried us through his undergraduate years at MIT, when the challenges of a rigorous academic environment tested his endurance. The same lesson stayed with us during his graduate studies, when his passions for theology and psychology intersected with his calling to teach and uplift others.

Today, when Jason shares his vision of helping students understand the psychological impact of racial injustice, we feel both humbled and proud. His work is his own, but it is also the fruit of years of planting, watering, and believing.

A Call to Action: Empowering Future Generations

The choices we make as parents and caregivers reverberate across generations. Too many bright young men and women, especially youth of color, are lost to the shadows of incarceration or to the quiet discouragement of low expectations. Their brilliance remains untapped, their contributions unrealized.

This loss is not only personal to the families involved; it is a societal tragedy. Imagine the breakthroughs in science, the art that could inspire, the innovations that could heal communities, if only those lives had been nurtured instead of neglected.

That is why we must prioritize our children's education over material distractions. The latest car or the newest designer clothes will fade. The investment in a child's mind and spirit will last forever.

And let me be clear—this responsibility does not rest solely on parents' and caregivers' shoulders. Teachers, mentors, faith leaders, neighbors, and policymakers, every adult who interacts with children carries a measure of this calling. Raising scholars is a collective project. It requires us to create schools where all students are seen, to build communities where curiosity is welcomed, and to model resilience, even when life is complicated.

Lessons in the Margins

- A child's success is rarely accidental; it is the result of consistent, intentional investment.

- Academic achievement is significant, but emotional intelligence and resilience are equally vital.

- Advocacy is not optional. When caregivers and communities speak up, children succeed.

- The sacrifices made today—time, resources, energy—become tomorrow's victories.

- Raising one scholar well can inspire many others; the ripple effect is real.

What Worked, What Didn't, and What Made All the Difference

What Worked

- Balancing academics with social and emotional growth, giving Jason both a strong foundation and the freedom to discover his passions.

- Advocating at key moments, reinforcing his confidence, and ensuring he was treated fairly, helping him stand tall in challenging environments.

What Didn't

- Leaning too heavily on academic achievement early on.

- Creative and extracurricular outlets took a back seat at first, though they later became essential as Jason matured and defined his own path.

What Made All the Difference

- Staying consistently involved—listening, guiding, advocating, and loving.

- The steady support of family, educators, friends, and mentors created a web of care that not only carried him through challenges but propelled him toward his purpose.

Strategy: 5 Ways to Invest in Your Children

Strategy	Why It Matters	How to Put It into Practice
Prioritize education over distractions.	Builds lifelong habits that value learning over short-term gratification.	Choose books, tutoring, and enrichment activities instead of fleeting material purchases.
Advocate relentlessly.	Ensures your child's needs and talents are recognized and supported within school systems.	Speak up at meetings, ask questions, and stand firm when your child's voice isn't heard.
Balance academics and creativity.	Encourages well-rounded growth and prevents burnout from overemphasis on grades.	Promote sports, arts, and hobbies alongside academics to nurture joy and confidence.
Model resilience.	Shows your child how to face challenges and recover from setbacks.	Share your own struggles and demonstrate how perseverance leads to growth.
Build a village.	Surrounds your child with support, mentorship, and positive influence.	Connect them with teachers, relatives, mentors, and community programs that reinforce shared values.

A Vision of Hope and Empowerment

As I close this journey, I return to where we began—the belief that children are not distractions from life's work; they are the work. The most critical work.

If we invest in them over time through advocacy, love, and unwavering belief, we can shape a generation prepared to lead with both intellect and heart.

This is not just my family's story. It is also a call to your family. Together, we can choose to raise scholars who are not only academically strong but also emotionally resilient, socially aware, and prepared to contribute to a better world.

The path forward is before us. Let us walk it with courage, purpose, and unity. For our children. For our future. *Scholars are raised, not left to chance.*

References

Chapter 1

National Early Literacy Panel. 2008. *Developing Early Literacy: Report of the National Early Literacy Panel.* Washington, DC: National Institute for Literacy.

Erdem, Cahit, and Metin, Kaya. "A Meta-Analysis of the Effect of Parental Involvement on Students' Academic Achievement." *Journal of Learning for Development* 7, no. 3 (2020): 367–83. https://www.jl4d.org/index.php/ejl4d/article/view/417.

Chapter 2

Chaparro, Juan, et al. 2020. *Early Childhood Care and Cognitive Development*, NBER Working Paper 26813. Cambridge, MA: National Bureau of Economic Research. http://www.nber.org/papers/w26813.

Hoyne, Caitríona, and Egan, Suzanne M. "Shared Book Reading in Early Childhood: A Review of Influential Factors and Developmental Benefits." *An Leanbh Óg* 12, no. 1 (2019): 77–92.

Johnson, M. Harris, and Munakata, Laura J. "Mechanisms of Learning and Plasticity in Childhood and Adolescence." *Annual Review of Psychology* 74 (2023): 197–220.

Williams, Margery. *The Classic Tale of Velveteen Rabbit Or, How Toys Become Real.* Illustrated by Michael Green. New York: Running Press, *1981.*

Chapter 3

Webb, Alexandra R. et al. "Mother's Voice and Heartbeat Sounds Elicit Auditory Plasticity in the Human Brain before Full Gestation." *Proceedings of the National Academy of Sciences* 112, no. 10 (2015): 3152–57.

Burgess, Stephen R. et al. "Cognitive and Environmental Predictors of Early Literacy Skills." *Reading and Writing* 15, no. 1 (2002): 93–120.

Chapter 4

Burgess, Stephen R. et al. "Cognitive and Environmental Predictors of Early Literacy Skills." *Reading and Writing* 15, no. 1 (2002): 93–120.

Silva, Natalia M., and Walker, Sheila M. "Children Need to See Themselves in Their Reading Material: Parental Perspectives on the Importance of Ethnically and Culturally Diverse Reading Material." *Journal of Children's Literature* 45, no. 2 (2019): 28–37.

Chapter 5

MacCann, Alexandra et al. "Emotional Intelligence Predicts Academic Performance: A Meta-Analysis." *Psychological Bulletin* 146, no. 2 (2020): 150–86.

Immordino-Yang et al. "We Feel, Therefore We Learn: The Relevance of Affective and Social Neuroscience to Education." *Mind, Brain, and Education* 1, no. 1 (2007): 3–10. https://doi.org/10.1111/j.1751-228X.2007.00004.x.

Chapter 6

Silva, Natalia M., and Walker, Sheila M. "Children Need to See Themselves in Their Reading Material: Parental Perspectives on the Importance of Ethnically and Culturally Diverse Reading Material." 28–37.

Hoyne, Caitríona, and Suzanne M. Egan. "Shared Book Reading in Early Childhood: A Review of Influential Factors and Developmental Benefits." 77–92.

Kaye, M. M. *The Far Pavilions.* New York: St. Martin's Press, 1978.

Keats, Ezra Jack. *The Snowy Day.* New York: Viking Press, 1962.

Rowling, J. K. *Harry Potter and the Sorcerer's Stone.* New York: Scholastic Press, 1998.

de la Peña, Matt. *Last Stop on Market Street.* Illustrated by Christian Robinson. New York: G. P. Putnam's Sons, 2015.

Palacio, R. J. *Wonder.* New York: Alfred A. Knopf, 2012.

Shetterly, Margot Lee. *Hidden Figures: The American Dream and the Untold Story of the Black Women Mathematicians Who Helped Win the Space Race.* New York: William Morrow, 2016.

Chapter 7
Dweck, C. S. *Mindset: The New Psychology of Success.* Random House, 2006.

Chapter 8
Herrera, Carla et al. "Mentoring with Elementary-Age Students: Impacts on Academic and Social Outcomes." *Child Development* 85, no. 2 (2014): 748–63.

Patel, Krupa et al. "MentorOn: A Peer Mentoring Program Developed for COVID-19 Times." *Journal of Community Psychology* 51, no. 3 (2023): 1500–15.

Chapter 10
Masri-Zada, Tariq et al. "The Impact of Social Media & Technology on Child and Adolescent Mental Health." *Journal of Psychiatry and Psychiatric Disorders* 9, no. 2 (2025): 111–30.

Chapter 11

Hemez, Paul et al. 2019. "Exploring the School-to-Prison Pipeline." *National Institutes of Health.* https://pmc.ncbi.nlm.nih.gov/articles/PMC8277150.

Chapter 12

Immordino-Yang et al. "We Feel, Therefore We Learn: The Relevance of Affective and Social Neuroscience to Education."

Cantor, Pamela et al. "Implications for Educational Practice of the Science of Learning and Development." *Applied Developmental Science* 24, no. 2 (2020): 97–140.

Chapter 13

Allensworth, Elaine M., and Clark, Kallie. "High School GPAs and ACT Scores as Predictors of College Completion." *Educational Researcher* 49, no. 3 (2020): 198–211. https://doi.org/10.3102/0013189X20902110.

Bettinger, Eric P. et al. "The Role of Application Assistance and Information in College Decisions: Results from the H&R Block FAFSA Experiment." *The Quarterly Journal of Economics* 127, no. 3 (2012): 1205–1242. https://doi.org/10.1093/qje/qjs017.

Carini, Robert M. et al. "Student Engagement and Student Learning: Testing the Linkages." *Research in Higher Education* 47, no. 1 (2006): 1–32. https://doi.org/10.1007/s11162-005-8150-9.

Chapter 14

Knoester, Matthew, and Au, Wayne. "Standardized Testing and School Segregation: Like Tinder for Fire?" *Race, Ethnicity and Education* 20, no. 1 (2017): 1–15, https://doi.org/10.1080/136133 24.2015.1121474.

Chapter 15

Choi, Yangsook. *The Name Jar*. New York: Alfred A. Knopf, 2001.

Lee, Harper. *To Kill a Mockingbird*. Philadelphia: J. B. Lippincott, 1960.

Wiesel, Elie. *Night*. Translated by Stella Rodway. New York: Hill and Wang, 1960.

Acknowledgments

To my siblings—Cicely, SallyAnn, Vere, Barbara, and Myra—thank you for carrying our shared story with honesty and love. You remain my first circle.

To my husband, Allison. Your patience and unwavering belief in me made this book possible. Thank you for walking with me through every chapter of this journey.

To Jason. Raising you has been one of my greatest joys. Your curiosity and determination inspired this book, and I am grateful for the privilege of being your mother.

To Cheryl Jaclin Isaac. Thank you for your thoughtful edits, gentle guidance, and the care you brought to every page. Your insight strengthened both the message and the manuscript.

To Victoria Wolf, Gokaran Singh Bohara, and all who contributed to the design and production process—thank you for treating this work with professionalism and respect.

And to every reader—thank you for inviting me into your home, your classroom, or your parenting journey. I hope these pages offer encouragement, clarity, and a renewed belief in what children can become when nurtured with intention and love.

About The Author

DR. JACQUELINE ASHE is an educator, wife, mother, and the founder of
Siblinks Publishing. She spent her career
in the New York City Department of
Education, serving students with diverse
learning needs and mentoring new
teachers with a calm, steady presence.

As a former special education teacher, Jacqueline's doctoral
research—*Empowering Middle School Students with Specific Learning
Disabilities to Complete Homework Successfully to Enhance Academic
Achievement*—reflects her lifelong commitment to helping children
thrive academically and emotionally. Her work blends research-
based insight with the cultural wisdom she carries from her
Caribbean upbringing and hands-on experience raising her son,
Jason, from early literacy to earning his PhD.

She teaches and supports women and families through her local
church community, where she facilitates weekly Bible study and
leads conversations about learning, legacy, and growth.

When she's not mentoring or building her next project, you can find Jacqueline baking her signature zucchini bread; crocheting blankets, scarves, and hats; cooking saltfish cakes in her kitchen; or enjoying videos of her grandson, AJ, discovering the joy of letters, numbers, and words.

Learn more about Jacqueline's work at raisingascholar.com.

Made in the USA
Middletown, DE
21 January 2026